HARRY GRATION'S YORKSHIRE SPORTING HEROES

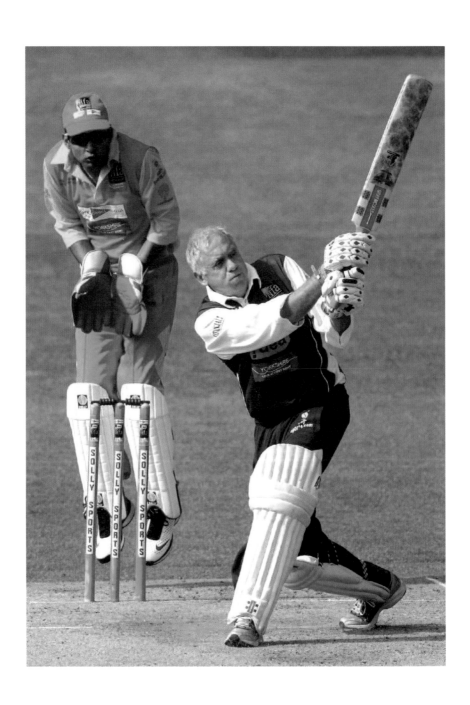

Harry Gration's Yorkshire Sporting Heroes

Dalesman

First published in 2009 by Dalesman
an imprint of
Country Publications Ltd
The Water Mill, Broughton Hall
Skipton, North Yorkshire BD23 3AG
www.dalesman.co.uk

ISBN 978-1-85568-268-9

Printed in China by Latitude Press Ltd.

Contents

Foreword
by Dickie Bird

I have been good mates with Harry now for over twenty years. No one enthuses about the county more than him. Harry is well known for being the presenter of *Look North* but for years he has worked on *Grandstand* and even presented it in the mid-1980s.

We got to know each other well when we made a documentary on my last season as an umpire. *Dickie Bird – A Rare Species* won a Royal Television Society award for top sports documentary in 1996.

For Harry's Yorkshire Sporting Heroes I love the idea of a top thirty and confess to be a little surprised by some of the top ten — not for their selection, but the order Harry has placed on them.

Above all, Harry has supported my foundation and many other charities with dedication for years.

If I wasn't so tight I'd buy this book!

Foreword
by Sir Michael Parkinson

Harry Gration is a delightful and professional journalist who other journalists admire. I know because I am a journalist and I admire him. He is also an agreeable and interesting companion which is a real bonus.

His book is about his love of sport and the people who play it. His choice of heroes is impeccable. Anyone who admires John Charles, Lewis Jones and Freddie Trueman, not to mention Geoff Boycott, Brian Close and Len Hutton, surely knows his onions.

This book will be read with joy by anyone who loves professional sport for what it really is — an entertainment and an antidote to the things that really do matter.

Writing about a couple of heroes, like John Charles and Len Hutton, he admits he never saw them play. He needn't worry, I did and can confirm his impeccable taste.

Preface

I have thought long and hard about the order of my top thirty Yorkshire Sporting Heroes. Talking to the *Yorkshire Post*'s Bill Bridge about it, he said he'd put money on Boycott being my number one. He isn't. My criteria was simple enough. Ability of course. Sportsmanship. Did they defy the odds? Would they have made the grade in any era? I hope my choices now look logical, if a little controversial as well.

Introduction

I have had a wonderful career (so far). My love affair with broadcasting began in the early 1970s and I will be forever grateful to two people who got me started.

While I was studying to be a history teacher — yes, me — I took a little-known course in television and radio. Next to sport, this was heaven for me. After I'd bent the ears of various Leeds United commentators, Doug Lupton took pity on me. He covered Leeds United matches for a new local station, BBC Radio Leeds. Now, Doug's wife worked for my dad who was manager of Boots the Chemist in York. (With me so far?) My dad had told Mrs Lupton that he had a nuisance of a son who, since the age of five, had ruined every cricket and football match he cared to watch by doing his version of a commentary. Someone had to tell him if this spotty, lanky nineteen-year-old had a chance, because Dad thought I had…

Me in the early days.

1

So, my introduction to real broadcasting had begun. Doug introduced me to the second person who got me started: John Helm, who was sports editor for the station. I couldn't have met a nicer bloke, a better friend, or a better tutor. Now, nearly forty years on, we are still best of pals.

My game-plan to become a broadcaster took a little diversion when I started working life as a teacher. This was really to satisfy my mum who wanted me to have a 'safe' job. But after five years I'd served my time. Don't get me wrong, I thoroughly enjoyed working at Rodillian School in Lofthouse as head of history at the age of twenty-five. But I always knew that the lure of broadcasting would one day win. That day came in 1978 when Radio Leeds offered me a three-month contract to work on general news and sport. It took me thirty seconds to make up my mind.

I threw myself into the job with a passion and was determined to make a success of it. My contract soon turned into a permanent post when I was made sports editor.

I stayed with Radio Leeds for four years before I was given a chance, out of the blue, to join BBC Television's regional news programme, *Look North*. Strangely, this happened because of an outside broadcast I did in York on the Pope's visit in the early 1980s. The news editor of the programme, Roger Bufton, is another to whom I owe a debt of gratitude as he saw in me a television potential I wasn't aware I had.

I loved working in television and was soon knocking on the door of *Grandstand* to see if I could work for them at weekends. It led to an astonishing few years. I presented *Grandstand* six times in 1986. *Match of the Day*,

Filming a sports outside broadcast for Look North.

Sportsnight and a *Grand Prix Special* followed. I went to Mexico in 1986 for the World Cup, to Edinburgh for the Commonwealth Games and then, my greatest experiences of all, five summer Olympic Games and three winter Olympics, which allowed me to travel all over the world.

Although I had a reasonable grounding in sports coverage, I still had to prove myself in London. The initiation process was a five-minute bulletin after *Grandstand* had finished. No one wanted to be involved in this — hardly surprising really when you consider that the flagship sports programme on BBC Television had probably been on air seven hours.

However that five-minute bulletin was the best preparation I could have had: I had to think on my feet, and

3

I have been fortunate enough to work at five summer Olympic Games, including Altanta in 1996 (top) and Sydney in 2000 (above).

If Pele had been born in or played in Yorkshire, I'm sure he would have been one of my Yorkshire Sporting Heroes.

ad-lib for my life. I loved it, and every Saturday for a year I would travel to London to do the programme. I honestly feel that experience was one of the most exciting of my life and I would not have missed it for the world.

I stayed with *Look North* until 1994 before taking a break from broadcasting to join the Rugby Football League. It was not a good move for me. The job was not what I had expected and I wanted out within months. I stayed a year, got the RFL £1.5 million in sponsorship, then returned to the world of broadcasting.

The problem for me, though, was that I was not used to set hours of work. Personally I found my boss Maurice Lindsay to be a challenging man and working with him was an experience, to put it mildly. I certainly wasn't used to being on call all the time and in truth we soon had a

On the set of Look North *with my colleague Christa Ackroyd.*

few interesting exchanges. To be fair to him he was trying to get major deals done in a sport which, I have to say, was very parochial. Whilst I never really got on with Maurice, I did have an appreciation of his determination. There were lots of other talented people there too, notably Sir Rodney Walker and Gary Hetherington spring to mind. Maurice was on a mission for the game of rugby league. Rupert Murdoch was desperate to get his hands on the sport and, crucially, turn it into a summer one. That was where the gap in Sky Sport's broadcasting was and for Maurice the sponsorship of rugby league by Sky Sports became his greatest achievement. Over £50 million came into the game and Super League was created. It made me realise, though, that it was not the kind of job I was comfortable in and I left at the first opportunity.

At Headingley rugby league ground, where I have spent many happy hours both working and as a spectator.

Initially, that was with the *Today* programme on Radio 4 and then, surprisingly, to *South Today*, *Look North*'s sister programme based in Southampton. I worked there just short of five years before my return to *Look North* at the end of 1999.

There's a book there somewhere, I am sure. This one, however, is something I have wanted to do for years.

My sporting heroes all have Yorkshire connections. I hope the lists provide some debate, with one or two controversial selections evident in each. But one thing is clear. Some of our sporting icons are incredibly special because they overcame so many odds. I suppose those are the ones I have leaned affectionately towards. I hope you enjoy my selections.

I

John Charles

If I have one regret in life it is this: I never really saw John Charles play at his best. I was certainly in the queue for the Leeds United 'Scratching Shed' on his return to the club when it doubled ticket prices to help pay for his transfer. I seem to remember that the entry price for adults was something like 7s 6d. There was an outcry, but the place was full. Those who did see him play all agree: he was the finest footballer of his generation. Even the great Jack Charlton, who wasn't easily impressed, concurred. This guy was special.

In the 1953-4 season Charles scored forty-three league and cup goals for Leeds. Strangely though, I think it is true to say that he was better known for the years he played away from these shores. He signed for Juventus in 1957 for a world-record fee of £65,000 and to this very day the club acknowledges the immense contribution he made. Hardly a surprise when you look at what he helped it achieve: three league titles. And Il Buone Gigante (the gentle giant) as he was known was never booked. He really was a bulk of a man — fourteen stones and well over six feet tall — and he could, and perhaps should, have bullied his way through his career. He never did.

Born in Swansea, Charles won thirty-eight caps for

John Charles — the finest footballer of his generation and my all-time Yorkshire Sporting Hero — turns out for Leeds United.

Wales and had an impressive goal tally of fifteen. He actually captained Wales to the quarter finals of the World Cup back in 1958. Indeed it was while playing for his country that he caught the eye of the Italians. On his debut as captain he was watched by the president of Juventus who was so impressed he made a bid to Leeds for the player. Leeds didn't want to sell their finest footballer, but were short of money. No change there then. (They had recently had their stand burned down.)

Charles was represented in the transfer talks by football commentator Kenneth Wolstenholme who had great contacts in Italy. The deal he clinched was fantastic by the standards of the day: a world-record fee for Leeds, and a £10,000 signing-on bonus for Charles. The norm was £10.

Many thought he would never live up to the build-up. But his impact was immediate. His goal-scoring talents in a league renowned for its defensive strengths were proof of his abilities, and secured his place in Italian hearts and history. His visits to Italy always brought a special welcome for him and twenty years after he had played his last game for the Juventus side, his diving header in the San Siro against AC Milan was still used in the credits for the Italian equivalent of *Match of the Day*.

I talked to John many times about the 'Italian job' and how it dramatically changed his life.

"When I first got there", he told me, "I couldn't understand their passion for football. I was recognised everywhere. And I mean everywhere. If I went out for a meal I hardly ever had to pay. I lived like a king and received fabulous bonuses. During one local derby when I could have scored a goal but the player I ripped the ball off was injured — I'd caught him accidentally with my elbow and knocked him out cold — so I stopped and kicked the ball

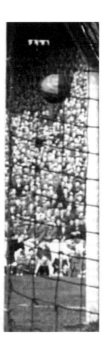

John Charles scores for Leeds against Bristol in the 1955-6 *season.*

into touch. The Juventus crowd went mad. But then, in an instant, applause rang round the ground. When I got home that night there were flowers in front of my car. Yes, I think they did quite like me."

What was his best goal? John had no doubt. "We were playing Fiorentina in a League Cup final in 1960. We were trailing and playing badly, losing 2-1. Then I got this cross. It hit my forehead and I controlled it, and as the keeper came out I headed it again over his head. I felt like a seal in a circus with a beach ball. How I did it I will never know."

When John returned to Leeds he came back with a heavy heart. His first marriage was in trouble and he was homesick too. It was sad that in his second stint at the Elland Road club he managed only eleven games before

Roma snapped him up for £70,000. This time, though, he had lost that edge. An injury to his knee made it a difficult period and he ended his career at Cardiff City, Hereford and Merthyr Tydfil.

Although he received the CBE in 2001 many thought that John had been overlooked. Certainly, when you talk about praise, two of football's greatest players — Nat Lofthouse and Billy Wright — without hesitation put John Charles right at the top. The love that the Italians had for John was demonstrated after he suffered a heart attack in Italy while promoting his book. Complications set in but Juventus had no hesitation in paying the hospital costs of £14,000 to get him back home to Yorkshire.

It is sad, isn't it, that we were not allowed to see Charles play in the modern game. Imagine what it must have been like to head the kind of football they played with in the 1950s and '60s. Jack Charlton once told me that on a very wet day it could take you minutes to come back to your senses.

John, who could play centre forward or centre half with utmost ease, told me:

"Yes, I could have played in this modern game. Imagine what I might have earned too. £20,000 a week at least."

More like £100,000 in all probability.

His funeral in Leeds was a magnificent tribute from the fans of Leeds. But there was much more to it than just that. I saw Cardiff, Juventus, Roma, Barnsley, Sheffield Wednesday and Sheffield United fans mingling in the crowds as the cortège made its way to Elland Road and then right round the ground.

Leeds United are not exactly the most popular side in Yorkshire but when the truly great depart there is a mutual respect that only football fans can deliver.

2
Geoffrey Boycott

My first meeting with Geoffrey Boycott was in 1972 at Park Avenue in Bradford. The initiation began immediately. At this stage I was working for Radio Leeds part-time. After asking him for an interview, he told me to carry his cricket bag into the dressing room. David Bairstow watched on, along with John Hampshire and Doug Padgett. I wondered why they were laughing.

"Thanks", said Geoffrey. "I might speak to you at close of play."

He didn't. Then I knew why.

I went through the same rigmarole a dozen times before he did grant me an interview. A relationship was slowly established, one which flourished during Yorkshire cricket's 'civil war' in the late 1970s and early 1980s when the powers-that-be wanted Boycott sacked. Here lay the core of Geoffrey Boycott's cynicism towards the media at this time. My support of his cause led me to a lifetime ban at Yorkshire (it lasted three days) and one or two torrid rows with a certain Freddie Trueman. Geoff's unhappiness was profound. The Yorkshire committee in those days was ridiculously large.

"Do you realise that those people, all twenty-seven of them idiots on the committee, sacked me two days after

My first meeting with Geoffrey Boycott in 1972 was inauspicious,
but we became firm friends.

Yet another four runs for Geoff playing for Yorkshire.

my mother died? I was distraught. The only county I ever wanted to play for did this to me."

The civil war in Yorkshire cricket is complicated, but stemmed from the county's lack of success and the need to blame someone for it.

Geoff and the Yorkshire cricket team (with another of my Yorkshire Sporting Heroes, David Bairstow, fourth from the left) at Headingley in 1971.

Now, Geoff is a different man. When my colleagues learned that I was to interview him in South Africa recently they said "Great place, shame about the interviewee". They couldn't have been further from the truth. The Boycott of 2009 is happy. He is funny and at ease that he has nothing to prove any more to anyone.

His house in Paarl near Cape Town on a beautiful golf estate is by anyone's standards fabulous. As we drank wine on his balcony and looked at the mountains I remarked that they looked like Malham.

"Aye, Harry, and if you have another bottle they look like Scarborough as well."

South Africa is special to him and the locals love him. They know his every whim: two eggs at lunch with salad; never toast his bread.

His first tour was to South Africa in 1964. "I hit a few decent knocks and made a good seventy to save a Test match."

Twenty-five years ago this year he took the famous rebel tour to the country. South Africa was banned from world cricket because of apartheid and, along with Chris Old and Arnie Sidebottom of Yorkshire and a cheque for £50,000, he defied the establishment and cemented a special bond with the people.

He is now one of only three VIPs at this golf estate. He has a private lounge which he can share with one of South Africa's richest men and F W de Klerk, the former president.

Nelson Mandela expressly asked to meet him a few years ago to say thank you for his support during the apartheid years. How ironic that Mandela's prison was only a mile from Geoff's pad in South Africa.

His demeanour, though, is so different to the one I experienced back in the 1980s. His wife clearly matches him.

Playing golf with Geoff is a good way to the new man. First I had to practise. I have never done that in my life. When I fluffed a chip, Geoff growled "You need to be committed to the shot." When he fluffed his putt moments later his wife quipped "So that is commitment is it, Geoff?" He laughed.

"I love golf", Geoff told me, "and I am better than a fourteen-handicapper. But these guys don't know about pressure. I know about that. Face Michael Holding from twenty-two yards — that's pressure."

Then he tells me it is time to practise my putting. His bluntness returns. "Golf is the only game I know where the worse you are the more hits you get." I certainly added weight to that debate.

His life in South Africa brings out the best in him and so does his involvement in Yorkshire cricket. He is now a member of the board. Listening to him speak you would think that he runs the club totally. But he does acknowledge with some respect a little help from Colin Graves, Robin Smith and Stewart Regan.

He enthused about what Darren Gough and Martyn Moxon gave to the club in 2008.

"Goughie smiles all the time. That is what I want to see at Yorkshire. We will miss him in the dressing room. We have won the Spirit of Cricket Award and, okay, it isn't the championship but it is a start. I want us to pay proper wages, not silly stuff and make people proud to play for us."

That has a familiar ring to it. There were times when Geoff hated playing for the club, I am sure. There were few smiles then.

The youngsters are at the heart of his commitment to the county. Johnny Bairstow may be a favourite but there'll be no favouritism shown to him. The young player has already made his first-team debut and made eighty-two not out. Not bad. But Geoff was critical.

"He was out recently playing a reverse sweep ... if he does that again he will get the biggest rollicking of his life. He also has to stop playing all these other games he is so good at like rugby union."

Geoff reminded me that he used to play for Leeds

United. So why now does he support Manchester United? The look he gave me told me I was perhaps pushing his new persona too far.

He wants to see all the youngsters given their chance.

"We have so much talent from quickies to spinners. Watch out for Adil Rashid. He'll make it too. We are getting there and I tell you this Jacques Rudolph is a smashing guy. Dead right for us."

So too is the way the county is run.

"I can remember playing for Yorkshire and Brian Close would be called off the pitch to attend a committee meet-

A snapshot of Geoff in the nets.

ing. When he came back, a lot of the lads were asking if they'd been picked for the next three matches. What a way to run the greatest cricket club in the world."

Much of his contentment these days, though, is the all-round acceptance he now feels he has.

"Obviously the cancer did change me, but I am in demand by everyone as a commentator ... a world-class one at that. But my daughter Emma makes me realise that I am nobody special when she is around."

His career highs?

"1965, the Gillette Cup final — 146, still the best ever score. My hundredth hundred of course and my Test

With Geoff on the golf course at his home near Cape Town.

match century comeback at Trent Bridge when I ran out Derek Randall."

I told him that the ovation for him at Headingley on his hundredth hundred was over seven minutes long. Staggering.

Yes, this is a different Geoffrey Boycott. But he can still call a spade a shovel when he has to.

"When you come out to Cape Town, Harry", he had asked me, "bring me a small parcel will you? They are my wife's new golf clubs."

To say they were bigger than his darned cricket bag would be an understatement. You see, some things never change.

3
Brian Close

He was one of the great captains in the history of cricket, with courage beyond belief and who was totally unselfish. Trevor Bailey once described him as possibly the greatest all-round talent he had ever seen. What a shame that the statistics don't really back this up.

He came onto the scene for Yorkshire in 1949 and, like Willie Watson, was also a very fine footballer. He had intended to go to university but the approaches of Leeds United and Yorkshire changed his direction.

For Yorkshire his progress was initially slow until 1949 when he was plunged straight into the county side for the matches against Oxford and Cambridge universities. He took twelve wickets and hit eighty-six runs which was enough to persuade the selectors at the county to give him another run.

He had a superb season and impressed so much that he found himself in the England team that faced New Zealand in the third Test at Old Trafford. Let's remember that this was Brian's first season and I cannot remember that happening before or since. But he is still the youngest ever to play for his country at 18 years 149 days.

Actually his Test match debut was hardly earth-shattering: one wicket for eighty-five runs and he was out third ball. He returned to Yorkshire where he completed the double of 100 wickets and 1,000 runs in the season.

Brian's first overseas tour was to Australia and turned out to be a defining moment. It established him in the eyes of the hierarchy as a troublemaker. He was nineteen at the time and even to this day talks of the shabby way he was treated by the captain and some of the officials. The tour was less than spectacular for him, and he found the pace of Ray Lindwall and Keith Miller too much for a young lad to handle.

The football side of his career fizzled out notably after what must be a unique situation. In 1952 the Yorkshire captain Norman Yardley gave Close permission to leave the season's opening game early so that he could play for Arsenal. But right at the last minute this permission was rescinded and, arriving late for the Arsenal game, Close was summarily dismissed. The end to his football career came in 1953 following a serious knee injury while playing for Bradford City.

He could now concentrate on his cricket career for Yorkshire. His first century didn't come until 1954, against the touring Pakistan team. Test match appearances were rare but he got one against South Africa in 1955 and then a call-up for the tour of Pakistan.

I suppose, though, that Brian will always be associated with controversy. The year 1961 produced a prime example. I can remember vividly listening to the drama as it unfolded on *Test Match Special*. England were set 256 to win in four hours at Old Trafford. Ted Dexter played a superbly fluent innings of seventy and Richie Benaud, trying to slow down the England momentum, started to bowl leg breaks in the rough. Close came in and promptly despatched Benaud for six but then tried to do it again

Brian Close was the one of the greatest cricket captains of all time — and without doubt one of the bravest. Here he is batting in the 1966 season.

and was out. The critics called him reckless. I talked to Benaud about this a few years ago.

"Brian Close should have been captain of England years before he was", Benaud told me, "and you know what people didn't realise was that he was trying to put me and the team off their game. It was a gamble so typical of Closey. You win some, you lose some."

He didn't become Yorkshire captain until 1963. The committee, perhaps sensing that the team's potential was

Yorkshire celebrate victory in 1960: Brian Close (with plaster on head) is in the centre, with Freddie Trueman to the right, and (seated) Ray Illingworth and Geoff Boycott.

Brian celebrating again with the Yorkshire team (including Geoff Boycott, second from right) on winning the 1963 County Championship at Grace Road, Leicester.

being seriously undermined by too many strong and dominant personalities, thought that Close could tame them. Championships flowed for the White Rose county again and, although the rows in the dressing room were at times the stuff of legend, Yorkshire's followers had a great leader once more.

The England selectors noticed Brian again, mainly because they were being brutally assaulted by the greatest fast bowlers ever to hit these shores. The West Indies had in their armoury Wes Hall and Charlie Griffiths. To this day Close's innings at Lord's will go down as one of the greatest in the history of the game. Chasing 234 to win, England found themselves at 31-3. Colin Cowdrey had broken his arm. Brian came in and took the short balls on his chest, arms ... anywhere. To unsettle the West Indians he even took guard down the pitch and, although he was eventually out for seventy, England survived for a draw. After scoring 300 runs in the series he was then dropped.

The day after his remarkable innings against the West Indies, Brian played for Yorkshire. Before the match a colour photo was taken in the dressing room of his injuries sustained the day before — and pictures of the bruises were soon on the front page of every newspaper. Once the photographers had done their bit, in typical blunt style Brian told them to clear off and let him get on with his job.

He bowled twenty-five overs, took six for fifty-five, and scored sixty-one as Yorkshire won another game on their way to winning the County Championship.

But England and Close still had a few chapters left. Notably 1966 and the return of the West Indies. By the time Close had been made captain for the fifth Test, the West Indies were three-nil up in the series. The return of Brian completely changed the whole attitude of the team in the dressing room and one pivotal moment was about to be added to Brian Close history. Sadly this incident doesn't exist on film or videotape any more due to part of the BBC library having been lost. So I will try to describe it for you.

The player of the series was Gary Sobers. He was averaging 100 when he came in and seemed so invincible that even Close felt that Sobers could win the game on his

Brian Close captained the Yorkshire team which won the 1966 County Championship, here pictured at the Oval. Back row, left to right: Waring, Sharpe, Binks, Wilson, Hutton, Hampshire, Padgett, Boycott. Front row: Illingworth, Close, Trueman, Taylor.

own. Brian, though, had noticed a weakness in the great man: the hook, especially early on. So, positioning himself at short leg, he ordered John Snow to drop one short and tempt Sobers to hook. It worked but only because, as Sobers flayed at the ball, Close refused to flinch. The ball took a nick onto his pad and Close took the catch. I would go so far as to say this: he is the only cricketer in the world who could have taken that catch.

Close was now supreme. Captain Marvel. He had one major ambition left. To lead the MCC abroad in a major tour. The year 1968 dawned and he was relishing the tour, especially after a series trouncing of Pakistan and India

27

earlier. The Yorkshire captain, though, had his detractors. Enemies is not too strong a word. They felt that his lack of diplomacy would lead to problems in the sensitive area of the world to which he was about to travel. Their opportunity to dispense with his services came in a most disgraceful way.

Yorkshire were facing Warwickshire in Birmingham and in difficult circumstances the home side were chasing victory. Yorkshire, though, only bowled twenty-four overs in 100 minutes (these days that is fast) and Warwickshire failed by nine runs. The upshot of this was a severe censure for Close, who refused to apologise, and ultimately the sack from the job he coveted the most.

It is still one of the most disgraceful decisions ever undertaken by the MCC and still hurts him bitterly.

His later career took him to Somerset where Vic Marks became one of his army of fans. But not immediately. Vic tells the story of being on the fringe of the first team and as twelfth man he had to do everything Close bid him to do — cups of tea by the gallon and so on. He even had to sand Closey's bat. He did this diligently because he knew what would happen if he didn't. After an age he finished the bat — only to be told that he'd done the wrong one.

But my favourite tale comes from another encounter with the great Gary Sobers. This time he strode to the wicket to face another great — Tom Cartwright, one of cricket's finest ever medium-pace bowlers. Brian ran over to Tom as he was about to deliver the first ball to the great Gary. What pearls of wisdom would come from Brian? Quite simply this: "He's a left-hander, Tom."

Yorkshire's loss was Somerset's gain. Big time. They started to win. But there was no hiding place for anyone who failed to reach Close's high standards. A one-day game summed up that so well. Leicestershire needed twelve to win off the last two balls. He wandered over to the fast bowler Alan Jones and told him exactly where he wanted him to bowl. Both deliveries were crashed over the boundary for six and an unlikely victory was plucked from the jaws of defeat. Close went straight for Jones at the end of the game and gave it to him full blast: "You stupid ★★★★★★ pillock. My mother could have done better than that."

For many years Yorkshire cricketers have felt that there has been a real bias against them. If we look at the way Close, Trueman, Illingworth and Boycott were treated at various times in their careers, their claims carry some weight.

My favourite Closey quote is simple but so true:

"I would have died for Yorkshire. Come to think of it, I probably did two or three times."

The year 2009 marked sixty years since Brian Close made his England debut. It passed without so much as a mention from him.

4
Billy Bremner

His statue stands outside Elland Road. It is the place where scarves are regularly placed as and when the moment arrives. I remember vividly covering Leeds United's European Champions League match in Istanbul when two supporters were murdered. Billy's shrine became the object of United's fans' respect for the murdered men. That is the esteem in which all Leeds fans hold 'the wee man'.

How good would Bremner have been in the modern game? I have no doubts that he would have been just as great. However, the nature of his game would have had to change. He was suspended far too often in his career and his combative style would have got him in untold trouble in these 'softer' times.

Billy gave everything for Leeds and Don Revie. I got to know him quite well over the years. As a player he summed up everything that was good about Leeds. To those many detractors during their glory years — and make no mistake, Leeds were hated by many — he epitomised why they were so disliked.

Bremner, though, had incredible talent. He never gave up, although in Paris in 1975 when Leeds had lost to Bayern Munich in the European Cup final he was in

Billy holds the 1969 Charity Shield; Leeds beat Manchester City 2-1.

tears. It was the end of the golden team. In truth it should probably have been broken up a year or so earlier.

In the early days of his life at Elland Road, Billy was a winger. He was eventually moved to midfield and became one of the most feared players in Europe. Eddie Gray told me that Billy was the one who would willingly change his role as the circumstances demanded.

"When we had a tough match away, like Liverpool or Manchester United", said Eddie, "the boss [Revie] would play Billy in a much deeper position. Almost a sweeper."

What I loved about Billy was that you could guarantee he would rattle up ten goals a season. I often marvel at the skills of Cesc Fabregas at Arsenal, but how many goals does he score in a season? You need that added dimension. Billy scored some truly great goals at vital times for his club. Against Celtic in the European Cup semi-final, and Manchester United in an FA Cup replay at Old Trafford, are two which spring to mind.

The story of Leeds though during those great years of the late 1960s and early '70s could well have broken many players. Before then they were a magnificent team, but fell well short of realising expectations. The League Cup final win in 1968 changed their fortunes and Billy won two Championship titles, the FA Cup and the Inter-Cities Fairs Cup. In 1974 Leeds won the Championship after going twenty-nine matches unbeaten; only Arsenal in 2004 have bettered that and they went through a whole season unbeaten.

I was personally surprised that he didn't enjoy outstanding success as a manager. His record was modest to say the least. He certainly did well at Doncaster Rovers on virtually no budget and was then given the job at Leeds United after Eddie Gray was sacked. He was in the job from 1985 to 1988 and the hope was that his passion for the game would ignite the players he inherited. In his first season he did quite well, stabilising a leaky defence, but the hopes of a promotion place were unrealistic. His best season was 1986-7 but, ironically, it led to his downfall. Leeds made the FA Cup semi-final at Hillsborough. I remember it so well because I had just fronted my first ever *Grandstand* the day before and raced up the motorway to watch the game sitting next to my mate Des Lynam. They lost this game despite taking an early lead.

But the real disappointment came in the league and the play-off failure against Charlton.

The next season Bremner was sacked. I was there covering the event for *Look North* and as Billy left the ground I expected his car to speed past without so much as a glance. He stopped the car, wound down the window and said to me, "It's life, Harry. I love this club but I didn't get it right. Another couple of months and I am convinced it would have worked."

Billy was, of course, the backbone of the Scotland team and it is probably no surprise that he was enmeshed in controversy at the end of it. He was playing in Copenhagen and, along with Willie Young, Joe Harper, Joe McCluskey and Leeds team-mate Arthur Graham, he was banned for life from international football. It was all to do with breaking a curfew and then an exchange later between Billy and an SFA official. The lifetime ban lasted one year but Bremner never added to his haul of fifty-four caps.

His death in December 1997 came just before his fifty-fifth birthday. The city of Leeds went into mourning and Sir Alex Ferguson no less came out of the funeral in Edlington, South Yorkshire, with tears in his eyes.

Leeds United's greatest player, in the eyes of the fans, is still sorely missed to this day.

5
Sir Len Hutton

I had the privilege of meeting Sir Len in London in 1984 six years before he died. At the time I had just started to get to grips with television and the need for patience when dealing with film crews. I should explain that most of our items then were done on film. It was never easy, unlike today with video, dvds or just mini-cassettes. To cut a long preamble short I interviewed the great man and was delighted with what we discussed. It was only on my return to Leeds that I discovered the film had jammed and I had no more than thirty seconds with him. I was devastated.

However, I do remember the things he told me: about what it meant to be a Yorkshireman, playing cricket for his county and being captain of his country.

"We were different to any other players", Sir Len said, "because we lived the game

Sir Len Hutton.

from morning to night. It was as if we had created our own religion. Others followed. We were the leaders."

Sir Len was a formidable leader. Indeed, when he died in 1990, my then boss Mark Byford made an incredible decision. Mark was always one for shocking us but he stood up quietly and said that Yorkshire had lost one of its greatest ever servants. The whole of the *Look North* programme would be devoted to Sir Len at his memorial service in York Minster.

I loved this opportunity.

Recently I got the chance to talk with Sir Bernard Ingham about all things Yorkshire. He was a great fan of Len and actually fulfilled one ambition for the county's greatest opening batsman by arranging a visit for him to No 10 to meet Margaret Thatcher. Apparently he was invited along with the cast of *Coronation Street*, and loved every minute of it.

Sir Bernard also recounts a quote from Richard Hutton, the son of Sir Len who of course played for Yorkshire and England: "I was introduced to my father when I was thirteen." I should add that there was no impropriety here, just an indication of how dedicated and committed he was to his career, and I suppose Yorkshire.

I think it is fair to say that Sir Len needed more than just cricket respect to become the complete person. He wanted his off-the-field behaviour to reflect what he was really like.

Len's career was always special. He made his debut for Yorkshire as a seventeen-year-old and in his first fourteen championship matches hit five half-centuries and one century (196 against Worcestershire).

His Test match debut followed in 1937 but it was the following year that established him as a national treasure.

In a stunning innings of thirteen hours he hit 364 against Australia at the Oval. Concentration became a byword for him but he could also play another way. Against the West Indies in 1939 he scored 196 at Lord's: the last ninety-six runs took him ninety minutes.

Had it not been for the war, during which he suffered a bad break in his arm, who knows what he would have achieved. His cricket was severely affected as a result and there are those who said that he was so concerned about his arm, which according to some accounts was two inches shorter, that it made him more cautious. He was only dropped once from the England team and that was against Bradman's wonderful 1948 touring team. There was disbelief in Yorkshire that such a thing could be done and local papers were full of letters saying how appalling it was.

I stumbled on a letter sent by my brother to the *Bradford Telegraph & Argus* about this very outrage:

"The England selectors quite simply do not know what they are doing leaving out the greatest opening batsman in the world. You will regret this decision mark my words."

Very astute of my brother and how true. Hutton was back in the team at the end of the series, scoring consistently if not spectacularly.

In the 1950s with Bradman retired, Len was number one and rattled off another double century against the West Indies. He became England's first professional captain in 1952 despite Yorkshire's continued insistence that they would only appoint amateurs.

His crowning glory must have been the 1954-5 tour of Australia when he led the team to a 3-1 series victory after losing heavily in the first Test at Brisbane. Mind you, it

*Len Hutton (right) with proud mentor Herbert Sutcliffe at the
1938 Scarborough Cricket Festival; earlier that same season, Len
had scored 364 against the Australians at the Oval.*

The cover drive was Len's 'signature' shot, and this pose will have been a familiar sight to many a weary bowler.

was a very good side indeed with the likes of Frank Tyson and Brian Statham as bowlers and young up-and-comers in the batting fold like Peter May and Colin Cowdrey.

Sir Len bowed out of the game in 1956 with a record to be proud of. As well as the 40,000 runs he made in his career, I think he gave the county so much to be proud of. No one deserved the tribute of a memorial service at York Minster more than he did. It was packed, with all the greats of the game past and present in the congregation.

The late great writer and broadcaster John Arlott summed up his career so well:

"He had all the grace that God could gift to a cricketer. His cover drive was venomous, but with beauty. He averaged very nearly a century every six innings."

Enough said.

6

Derek Dooley

I never saw Derek play, but as his playing career was tragically brief, I am not alone there. I use the word 'tragic' very sparingly in sport. It should only refer to loss of life. But in the case of Derek, who lost his leg at the age of twenty-three, I think it is the right word.

Talking to those who did see him play I have often heard comments on how, almost overnight, he transformed himself from a clumsy and awkward player to a deadly centre forward and one who was very difficult for defenders to play against.

There are very few people in sport who can attract affection from a city with two football teams. Denis Law springs to mind as a Manchester United player and later Manchester City. Derek Dooley did the same in Sheffield.

I have known to my cost that the people of Sheffield, and especially its football supporters, are passionate about their game. In fact, that's rather an understatement: like saying Romeo had a crush on Juliet. But when you look at the circumstances surrounding Derek's career it becomes even more of an achievement. I mentioned earlier that, when it comes to gaining respect, football fans are the hardest to please. At Derek's funeral in 2008 you could hear a pin drop as both Wednesday and United

Derek Dooley was a great servant to football, and particularly the two Sheffield clubs, United and Wednesday; at his funeral, both sets of supporters lined the streets to pay their respects.

supporters lined the streets to the cathedral and then broke out in spontaneous applause as his coffin was carried into the church. I confess I was moved to tears by this.

Derek was the son of a steelworker. You can imagine where he learned his trade. The local pitch was sparse of grass but had a luxurious covering of cinders and ashes. It made him tough and he eventually caught the eye of Sheffield Wednesday, turning professional in 1947. Most agree that the early part of his career was hardly impressive. In fact, it looked as if he was way out of his depth.

"Here I am at eighteen", Derek said, "when I was just starting to make some progress with Wednesday but it was interrupted by the arrival of my call-up papers, which meant two years in the RAF."

But in October 1951 something changed. Wednesday's manager was Eric Taylor. The Owls were struggling near the foot of Division Two (the Championship as it is called these days). Taylor needed a win to counter the pressure that was mounting on him. Barnsley were the opponents. They were a very physical outfit, but Dooley rattled in two goals and Wednesday beat their great rivals to start a remarkable surge up the league. Dooley went on the rampage too. By the end of the season, Wednesday were top and about to re-enter the top flight.

This of course was Derek's big chance. Between September and February he knocked in sixteen goals. Then came Valentine's Day in 1953. Wednesday went to Deepdale to face Preston. One of my uncles, now sadly departed, was a big Wednesday fan and was at the game.

"I never thought it was anything more than a run-of-the-mill injury", my uncle told me. "Albert Quixhall sent a super through-ball. Derek was on it like a flash, but so too was the Preston keeper George Thompson. Derek was flattened and clearly in agony."

The injury itself wasn't too bad — a broken shinbone. However, an infection set in at the back of the calf. It turned to gangrene and at one stage threatened his life. His leg was amputated. I talked to Derek about this moment after he made the BBC Yorkshire Hall of Fame a few years ago.

"Obviously I was shattered", said Derek. "But not for myself. I had only been married for six months. I suddenly realised I had no house and no trade to fall back on. That was my moment of despair. I then read an article in the *Sheffield Star* which made me cry — it said something like I was about to be selected for England. My God how I'd wanted that."

It took Derek nearly ten years to get a job back at Wednesday. There is a famous quote attributed to him: "I would be a corner flag for Wednesday if they'll have me."

Gradually, however, he became the cornerstone of the club. From youth team manager in 1962, he helped make Hillsborough one of the best grounds in the country as manager of the club lottery.

He became manager in 1971 and for a while it all looked good. Early season form put them top in 1972-3 but then came a slump; they eventually finished tenth that season. The next season, 1973-4, a mystery virus decimated the team and relegation looked likely. The bombshell came on Christmas Eve in 1973. He was sacked. For the first time in his life he was bitter towards the club he would have died for, indeed nearly did.

"I vowed then that I would never go back to Hillsborough under any circumstances."

For twenty years that vow held firm.

But his move to Sheffield United eventually made him change his resolve. He made his way up to chief executive and then chairman, and then in 1992 returned to Hillsborough for a derby match. The standing ovation he received from both sets of fans made him realise that his place in Sheffield history was unique.

At United he had a wonderful relationship with Dave Bassett and especially Neil Warnock. They were good years too, culminating in the Blades' promotion to the Premiership. Derek gave the club an added dignity and he was a great foil to Warnock. The United manager was a volatile character but in his chairman he had a calming influence who could defuse some of the problems he had created.

A truly special sportsman.

7
Neil Fox

The Fox brothers from Sharlston, a pit village in Yorkshire, must have been a handful to bring up. There was Don, famous of course for Eddie Waring's classic "poor lad" comment in the Watersplash Final of 1968 and another of my Yorkshire Sporting Heroes; Peter, who signed for Featherstone Rovers; and Neil, who went straight to Wakefield Trinity.

Alongside Lewis Jones, Neil can rightly be judged as one of the gods of the game. The record books groan with the weight of his achievements: 6,220 points, 358 tries and, wait for this, 2,574 goals.

During his career he played for six teams and was player-coach for Wellington in New Zealand; truly versatile, he started life in the centres and ended as a forward. For a decade he was first choice in the centre for Great Britain and his twenty-nine Tests showed just how much he had stamped his quality and class on the game.

I remember many years ago seeing a feature on Neil by Eddie Waring on *Grandstand*. It was all to do with kicking and in particular how difficult the old leather ball was to play with, particularly when saturated with rain. I seem to recall it was Joe Lydon of Wigan who was asked to kick the old-style ball using the more modern kicking

The Fox brothers are arguably one of the finest of rugby league dynasties; from left to right, Peter, Don and Neil.

technique and he nearly broke his foot in taking a shot at goal from the touchline.

Neil signed for Wakefield Trinity at the age of sixteen and made his debut against Keighley at just seventeen. Even more memorable was the part he played in beating the touring Aussies later in that season. Wakefield won 17-12 and Neil kicked four goals. If you read the *Wakefield Express* report of that game the paper said that two of Neil's touchline kicks, in thick mud, were some of the best ever seen at Belle Vue. In the years to come they became regular events.

In a career that spanned twenty years it is difficult to pick out one season above another. But if you look at

Neil Fox with the Challenge Cup. With Neil scoring tries and kicking goals from all parts of the pitch, Wakefield Trinity were a powerhouse in the game of rugby league in the 1960s and won the Challenge Cup three times between 1960 and 1963.

1957-8 the contribution that he made to Wakefield was exceptional. Trinity had to play five matches in two weeks — how impossible would that be today? In those games Trinity scored over 200 points and Neil contributed a staggering 106.

If you compare Neil's record with that of Lewis Jones then you can see they were almost toe to toe. Neil landed 124 goals and scored thirty-two tries.

When Neil left Belle Vue these were his records: twelve

Neil Fox (left) and his brother Don (right) with Carl Dooler (centre) were all winners of the Lance Todd Trophy awarded to the best player in a Challenge Cup final — Neil in 1962 for Wakefield, Don in 1968 for Wakefield, and Carl in 1967 for Featherstone — and moreover all three were from the same little pit village of Sharlston.

goals in a match against Batley in 1967; thirty-three points in the same match; 163 goals in a season, 1961-2; and 407 points in a season the same year.

The 1960 Challenge Cup final, when Neil was just twenty-one, saw him kick seven goals and score two tries as Trinity demolished Hull 38-5 — a twenty-one point haul. During this rich seam Wakefield were one of the forces in the game. Two years later Neil won the Lance Todd Trophy in the 12-6 success over Huddersfield. On this day he kicked three drop goals and scored a try. The very next year Trinity beat Wigan 25-10.

It seemed totally fair that Neil was made club captain the next year. But his form suffered and he asked to be relieved. In the next two years, however, his confidence returned and the side won their two championships. He was injured for the match against Leeds in 1968 when his brother Don won the Lance Todd Trophy (and, of course, missed that sitter in front of goal in the dying seconds).

His life at Wakefield temporarily ended in the following year when he signed for Bradford Northern, but that proved to be short-lived. He returned and played for the club he loved until 1974, before heading for Hull KR as a player and coach. He also had stints with York, Bramley, Huddersfield and Bradford again.

I was a regular at Clarence Street in York for many years and the excitement of Neil's signing for the so-called 'Steam Pigs' led to one of the biggest crowds for years at the ground.

8

Lewis Jones

Lewis Jones has got to be one of the gods of rugby league. I have never heard anyone say a bad thing about him. He oozed class.

In the background of course was the rivalry that existed between league and union in the 1950s. As a union player with Llanelli he was already the golden boy. As a teenager, he had forced his way into the Wales squad for the Five Nations back in 1950. His conversion, or betrayal, to league saw him dominate the game for nearly twelve years between 1952 and 1964. But it did come at a price. For many years he was shunned in Wales, and the authorities barely recognised his existence. They knew what they had lost.

Few players make an instant impact at international level. They usually grow into their role and as experience is attained they begin to show their class. Lewis is the exception.

However, the start of his career was remarkable because it was so ordinary. His call-up to international level seems quaint by modern-day standards. He recalls the letter he received. Bear in mind that Lewis, on leave from the navy, had never been to London let alone the headquarters of the Rugby Football Union. The letter read:

50

"You have been selected to represent Wales in the international match against England at Twickenham on Saturday Jan 21st 1950. The match kicks off at 3pm. You are requested to arrive by 1pm at the latest. Please bring your own boots. Shirt, shorts and socks will be provided and it is expected that you will return your socks and shorts at the end of the match."

Getting to the ground was even more bizarre. Nowadays of course there would be overnights in a top London hotel, coach travel and so on. Not in 1950. Lewis got the train from Cardiff along with all the hundreds of fans and went virtually unnoticed because he'd played most of his rugby outside Cardiff. He followed the crowds to Twickenham and then peeled off when he got to the players' entrance.

If he arrived there as a nobody, by 5pm it was all very different.

"I remember two things about the first half", said Lewis. "One was a tackle, not the strongest part of my game, on the England winger. The second happened minutes before half-time and I still wonder if I actually dreamed the whole thing. I got the ball just on my own twenty-five. I saw a gap and fifty yards later no one had come anywhere near me. I kept thinking 'I can kick for touch' [there were no restrictions or penalties in those days] and then I passed to Davies who scored. I later added a conversion and penalty, and remember being carried shoulder high off the pitch at the end."

What a year it turned out to be for him. At eighteen he was not expected to make the Lions squad for New Zealand, but an injury to an Irish player got him a late call up. He travelled to New Zealand by himself — it took nearly five days with elongated stop-overs. He played his

Lewis Jones — one of the true greats of rugby league.

first match the day after he arrived and it seemed that the world of rugby union had found a star who would be around for years. Then came the defection. He signed for Leeds for £6,000, a princely sum in those days, and was immediately tied to the Headingley club with an astonishing nine-year contract.

He was the total rugby league player. He was an incredible kicker, he could use searing pace to double-kick his way from tackles and chasers, and had one of the finest passing abilities ever seen.

For all of this talent, Leeds hardly took advantage in the silverware stakes. In truth his early start was lacklustre. He broke an arm and missed much of his first season. But those who know the game will tell you that the style of rugby played at Headingley during his time was of the highest standard. It was entertaining, if lacking from time to time in a ruthless streak which would have netted far more trophies.

Two medals are priceless to Lewis: that won in 1957 with Leeds at Wembley in the Challenge Cup final; and that in 1961 when Leeds won the Championship final. If you talk to anyone about the latter, and believe me they still talk about it, everyone refers to it as the Lewis Jones masterclass. They recall his fabulous jinking run at the end of the game which sealed what was always the holy grail for the Leeds club.

Statistics sometimes don't tell the whole story of a person's career, but in Lewis's case they do make impressive reading. Thirteen goals in one match, 166 goals in a season, 1,244 goals in his career and 431 in one season. But I think it is best to put all of these in context by looking at one season in particular. In 1956-7, he scored 496 points made up of thirty-six tries (three points in those

53

days) and 194 goals. Throughout his career he averaged just short of eight points a game for the club.

What I admire about this man is the humility he always portrays. He is at times dismissive about his talent, although no one around him lets him get away with that. Peter Fox the former Great Britain coach said: "You couldn't catch him. He was like a whippet, but so graceful. As good as my kid brother, Neil."

Lewis is still seen regularly at Headingley and can glide through a crowd with the same class he showed over fifty years ago. Strangely he only gained fifteen Great Britain caps and for some reason seems to have been made the scapegoat for a very poor showing by Great Britain in the 1957 World Cup against the Aussies. But he does hold membership in a very exclusive club. A Lion in union and in league.

He is also a very good golfer, playing off a single-figure handicap in his pomp. I won't be playing him.

9
Ray Illingworth

Leaving aside the fact that Ray was regarded as the enemy of the peace at Yorkshire, let no one be in any doubt that he was a brilliant captain of the England team. Indeed, there are those who feel that tactically he was in a class of his own. Some say he was England's finest captain after the Second World War. I would not disagree.

I think it is fair to say that the hallmark of a great captain is how he performs against the Australians. Michael Vaughan can certainly claim to be in the upper echelons after that fabulous success in 2005, but to beat the Aussies on their home soil is even more significant.

The year was 1971 and the England team was unbeaten in Test matches on the entire tour. Ray speaks fondly

Ray Illingworth.

about that time, even though it was a far cry from the kind of trip our current players enjoy:

"I didn't get on with the manager David Clark from the word go. He was a gentleman farmer and wanted Colin Cowdrey as captain. Instead he got me. A gruff, plain-speaking tyke."

Illy also remembers being given £25 expenses for the whole tour. "Do you know how long that lasted? One night in the bar before we set off."

The tour is remembered for the outstanding team spirit that Ray brought to the team. He has particular praise for Geoff Boycott and John Snow.

"Boycott had a fabulous tour. He made over 650 runs in the series and he missed the last Test because of a broken arm. He played for the team and scored runs quickly. For me he was easily the best opener in the world during this series. We got on fine."

Those remarks contrast sharply of course with events that happened ten years later at Yorkshire, but there has always been respect between the two for each other's abilities.

The other player singled out by Ray on that tour was the Sussex opening bowler.

"John Snow was quite brilliant. He bowled really fast and regularly turned the batsmen inside out, moving the ball off the seam."

I remember speaking to Ray not long after Michael Vaughan's Ashes success in 2005 about the celebrations which we all saw on television. Who can ever forget that picture of Andrew Flintoff staggering off the open-top bus twenty-four hours after the parade and still showing signs of being under the influence? A year later England went to Australia and were annihilated, and Flintoff's

Ray Illingworth, a brilliant cricketer and tactically astute captain.

off-field antics were criticised while he was captain. Ray points out that his touring party may well have liked a drink but would never have crossed the line.

"Had any of them not performed to their best ability and if I had found out they had been out drinking the night before a game, they would have been told and would not have played."

The strongest team Illy could field on that tour was Boycott, Edrich, Luckhurst, Fletcher, Illingworth, Knott, Underwood, D'Oliveira, Lever, Willis and Snow.

Ray captained England for thirty-one out of his sixty-one Test matches. He stepped down from the role after the West Indies trounced England in 1973. The third Test will live long in his memory I am sure. The match was played at Lord's and ended in a massive defeat by an innings and 226 runs. Both Rohan Kanhai and the great Gary Sobers hit 150. It was a sad end for Illy's career as captain but believe me, alongside Brian Close, we have never had a better leader.

I am often reminded of his instinct as a captain when he arrived at Grace Road in 1969 to lead Leicestershire. It is said that he took a look at the ground and asked for the boundary to be extended and the pitches made harder.

He had come from a very tough school at Yorkshire and it was generally accepted that he had little love for the way he was treated in the early part of his career. In particular, he suffered at the hands of Johnny Wardle and Bob Appleyard who were well known for not liking any catches being dropped off their bowling. Illy was also made to know his place. Appleyard had choice of ends and that was that. But in a strange way it was also the making of him. Wardle actually liked him in the end, mainly because Illy stood up to him and openly rowed with him if the

Ray introduces the Queen to the England team before their match against the West Indies at Lord's in 1969.

occasion demanded it. Indeed, he took over thirty catches off Wardle's bowling in one season.

He had to wait a long time for his Test debut — 1958 in fact — but when it came he bowled forty-five overs against New Zealand at Old Trafford and finished with 3-59.

I have already touched on the acrimony surrounding his return to Yorkshire during the Yorkshire 'civil war'. But his last eighteen months in cricket for the county actually did bring stability. Yorkshire won the John Player Trophy — a competition which would have been derided years earlier but which showed just how outstanding a captain he was. I was working for *Look North* by this stage and we covered the triumph as if England had won the World Cup. Illy allowed himself the chance to smile for the first time in months. I looked back at the archive recently and replayed the interview I did with him, with the trophy in his hand.

"I never thought I would get such a buzz from winning this competition", Illy told me. "But I can tell you it feels, after all the county has been through, as if we have won the championship and a Test series in one."

During this time when the Boycott supporters gave him and his family a hard time, he was suspicious of the media. He categorised me as 'Boycott's number one fan' and gave me very little. I don't really blame him for that. The silly thing is that he then became the victim of the Yorkshire cricket debacle. His contract was not renewed when the new committee took office after the special general meeting at Harrogate in 1984.

Ray Illingworth still eats and sleeps cricket. He looks after Farsley Cricket Club. This is so apt in many ways. As a fifteen-year-old he played for Farsley's first team in the Bradford League and made 148 not out in the league's Priestley Cup competition, an innings spread over a number of evenings. These days he is the groundsman/ secretary/just about everything. Let's be straight about this: how many former England captains, not to mention coach/managers, do you know who are still prepared to give as much back to cricket as they got from it?

I admire Illy enormously for this.

If you don't believe me, get along to Farsley early one morning and see him at his work.

10
Tony Currie

It seems inconceivable how a talent so rich could be overlooked by one of the top teams in the land. But that is exactly what happened to Tony Currie. Chelsea thought he did not have what it takes to become a top-class player. How wrong they were.

Full credit, then, to Sheffield United for seeing in Tony something they could develop. He was a brilliant player to watch and I have often thought how suited he would have been to the game now. Imagine him playing for Arsenal, or Manchester United, in midfield. What a dimension he would have given them.

He gave the Blades so much in his eight years at the club and cost a mere £26,500, bought

Tony Currie, a Blades legend.

Tony Currie in full flight for Leeds against Middlesbrough.

from Watford. How cheap does that sound in this day and age? He scored on his debut against Tottenham Hotspur. I can remember it to this day — a header. He then missed the next game because he got married.

In truth he stood out by a mile in a side that always struggled to survive in the top flight at the time. But

Blades fans agree that it was a privilege to watch him dominate a game. He played over 300 matches for Sheffield United and scored a respectable fifty-five goals. When he was sold for £250,000 to Leeds you can imagine how Blades fans felt. The rivalry between the two cities is intense.

For Leeds he was playing in a fading team. They had just lost the 1975 European Cup final and the old guard were being moved out. He replaced the great Johnny Giles and many Leeds fans were reluctant to welcome him in that role. It didn't take them long to realise what they had got.

I can recall, while working for Radio Leeds back in the mid-1970s, covering a story about the possible move of TC, as he was known, to Elland Road at the end of 1974. The Bremner/Giles duo was still a force but they were getting on. I have always felt that, had he moved then, Leeds would probably have won the European Cup in Paris in 1975.

While at Leeds I thought he played the best football of his career. Leeds reached the League Cup semi-finals in 1978 and '79, and also finished fifth in the league to qualify for Europe. He left the club after a series of disputes with manager Jimmy Adamson with the Leeds side playing some of the worst football in its history.

While at Bramall Lane in 1972 the then England manager Sir Alf Ramsey had given him his first international cap. It wasn't a success because, along with a certain Rodney Marsh, the team looked too silky-skilled for many and Northern Ireland beat England 1-0.

He got another chance when England beat Austria 7-0 in September 1973. Currie scored and showed something of what was needed by the team. He then played in that

Tony is honoured by Sheffield United for his many years of loyal service to the club.

never-to-be-forgotten match at Wembley in 1974 when England simply had to beat Poland to qualify for the World Cup finals in Germany. It is still one of the most incredible results and was a devastating blow for England. To make sure that the attacking nature of the side was underlined, Currie was picked and helped his team totally dominate the game. But the exploits of the Polish goalkeeper, who Brian Clough called a "clown", denied England and a dreadful mistake by Leeds United's Norman Hunter ensured that the World Cup winners of 1966 would not be in the main event just eight years later.

After Leeds, Tony moved to Queens Park Rangers for £400,000, but from this point his career was blighted by injuries and we never saw the same silky skills apart from the odd game. He did share one great moment, captaining Rangers in the 1982 FA Cup final replay, but after eighty-one games for the club he dropped out of league football.

He is remembered by me with a very simple piece of commentary from John Motson during a game between Sheffield United and West Ham: "A quality goal from a quality player."

A perfect description.

I I

Fred Trueman

My love of cricket began in my home city, Bradford. My dad and brother used to take me to matches at Park Avenue. Indeed, my football team was always Avenue rather than City, and for me the twin ground of football and cricket was a real highlight to visit. Its loss was a real blow to the city, something I will deal with later in the chapter on my favourite Yorkshire sporting grounds.

I played cricket a lot as a young lad and there was no doubting who my hero was: Fiery Fred. I loved his beautiful bowling action. To me it was so smooth and yet devastating. This is where grounds like Park Avenue came into their own. You got the best view of your heroes — something which modern grounds deny you today.

When Yorkshire played at Park Avenue in my school holidays, my brother and I could spend the whole day watching the cricket and my dad would come along at the end of his day and pick us up.

Why was Park Avenue so special? Easy. You could run round the ground and pat the players on the back as they came out and then play cricket on the pitch. When Fred came out to bat there were always loads of kids jostling for the best position to wish him luck.

I often wonder how Fred would have fared in the

Facing Fiery Fred in his pomp must have been an unnerving experience for batsmen all over the world. This photograph gives a vivid impression of how the Australian batsmen saw the twenty-two-year-old Fred in the Test series of 1953.

cricket we play these days. Indeed, I asked him that very question just a few months before his untimely death.

"I'd have been just as good — probably better", he replied. That of course was the real strength of Fred.

"I knew I could bowl out anyone, lad. No one frightened me and I got some fabulous scalps in my career like Sobers, Worrell, Pollock and Richards, not to mention all those Aussies."

Indeed the Aussies brought out the best from Fred. He recalled his 1953 Ashes Test appearance when England beat the Australians at the Oval to secure the series.

"It was all to play for with the first four Tests having been drawn. I got a place back in the side. I should have been in all of those Tests anyway. I took four wickets in the first innings, and then Tony Lock and Jim Laker bowled them out in the second innings for us to win the series."

For Fred those memories were so special and a lot of people didn't realise that the night before the match started his grandmother died. He nearly pulled out. Afterwards he remembered the celebrations.

"I will tell you it was nowt like that 2005 lot. We had a cake and some champagne, and then I was handed a telegram telling me to return immediately to my RAF station and report back for duty at 9am the following morning. How is that for coming back to reality?"

He received £75 for that historic success.

It is worth remembering just who were responsible for that incredible achievement in 1953. This was the team: Len Hutton, Bill Edrich, Peter May, Denis Compton, Tom Graveney, Trevor Bailey, Godfrey Evans, Jim Laker, Tony Lock, Alec Bedser and Fred.

Can you imagine what it must have been like to have a team like that and be a part of it?

My relationship with Fred was not good during the Boycott years at Yorkshire. He was angry at my support of Geoff but his own attitude to him actually turned overnight. News of Geoff's serious illness prompted Fred to call him. The years of animosity disappeared immediately. They became really good friends and for me it was one of the truly great moments of sport. Both acknowledged each other's abilities but now a mutual bond emerged which was genuine. I have no doubt that Fred's support of Boycott helped him immensely during his dark hours.

I often went to dinners and heard Fred speak. He captivated his audience with that down-to-earth Yorkshire grit.

One story always intrigued me. It is said that in one benefit match in the 1960s Fred was bowling fairly gently in the game when in came a well-dressed batsman wearing a cravat. Fred didn't like cravats. He bowled the first delivery and there was a clear edge to the wicket keeper. "Not out" said the umpire. The second was more hostile and trapped the poor batsman leg before. Not out again. By this time Fred was incensed and unleashed one of his specials, with the middle stump cartwheeling past the slips.

Before the umpire could utter a word Fred turned to him and said: "I nearly had 'im there, didn't I?"

He played many games against the universities of Oxford and Cambridge. They were usually great opportunities to collect cheap wickets. One such occasion saw a very distinguished player enter to face the bluntness of Yorkshire and Fred at their pomp. He was elegantly dressed, and played some beautiful cover drives before taking his guard. After what seemed an eternity the umpire

Fred Trueman was a hero to me and many other young lads.

shouted "play" and Fred unleashed a superb delivery which knocked out the middle stump of the aristocrat.

"Well bowled, Freddie", he exclaimed.

"Aye lad, but it was wasted on thee."

He also engaged in psychological warfare. A visit to the opposing team's dressing room would give him a chance to glare at the team and say "I fancy five or six today, especially on this wicket."

Then, of course, there was his habit, when going out to field, of hanging back and as the two opening batsmen opened the gate, he was there with advice.

"Don't close the gate. You'll be back before you know."

He loved working for *Test Match Special*. It hurt him badly when they started to phase him out. He never really got over that. But he was brilliant as a summariser, if increasingly caustic as the years rolled on.

I was listening to a tape recently looking back on the Headingley Test match which was abandoned after protestors scarred the wicket in 1975. It was all to do with a prisoner called George Davis. The match was beautifully poised and had seen the unfortunate Keith Fletcher drop a number of easy slip catches. As ever Fred's very forthright views came over.

"I would have all those protestors lined up on the pavilion roof and throw them off with Keith Fletcher down below to catch them."

Geoff Cope, who played for Yorkshire with distinction in the 1970s and '80s, told me one great tale about Fred at Bramall Lane. It was one of those wickets on which you didn't really want to be facing him. Yorkshire were playing Surrey and, with a couple of early wickets, Fiery was relishing the arrival of the incoming batsman, Micky Stewart. The first ball hit him just under the heart.

Micky went down the pitch, prodded it and returned to face the next offering. This whistled past his nose and another venture down the wicket brought a more venomous prod on the offending area. Micky survived another torrid over but his gardening started to attract comments of discontent from a few of the characters in the crowd. Another over and Micky was again hit in the chest. He went down the wicket and attacked the divot with ferocity. Then came the comment:

"Careful, Micky. If tha hits it any harder, wicket will collapse and there are men working under there."

Priceless.

One of the saddest aspects of Fred's life for me was that he genuinely felt that the county he loved cared little for him. This was shown in the structure of pay and in how he was treated in the pecking order. He said he never received anything from Yorkshire to recognise his 300th Test match wicket. That is a disgrace. Fred's attitude to the club was clearly nurtured by what happened to him in those early years. But he was never, perhaps surprisingly, critical of the hierarchy. He always spoke highly of Norman Yardley, although many others did not. But in recent times his contributions have been recognised. He would definitely have been made president of the club at some stage.

Twenty astonishing years in his career, with over 2,300 wickets, but one statistic that would make our current crop of quick bowlers cringe with disbelief. He had bowled over 16,000 overs — or nearly 100,000 deliveries. Some of the fast bowlers these days only bowl 200 overs in a year.

It was significant that Fred chose Bramall Lane for his swansong back in 1968. I always fancied myself as a fast bowler. In '68 I was about to become captain of St Peter's

School cricket team, and I jumped at the chance to go to Sheffield to see my hero in action and with the intention of watching how a captain actually inspired his team on the pitch.

The match itself was an amazing climax for Fred. Yorkshire beat the Aussies by an innings and sixty runs, with Fred taking wickets and making runs. He also took a fabulous catch at gully to dismiss Doug Walters.

But one memory abides from that day and brought me to tears. I was not alone either. The sight of Fiery Fred running in one last time from his full run. As John Arlott so beautifully described it.

"The mounting glory of rhythm, power and majesty, then the release of momentum, pace and problems for the batsman."

His death on 1st July 2006 occurred during a Test match at Headingley against the West Indies. Ray Illingworth and Brian Close were both in tears. The warriors who shared so many great Yorkshire moments and, no doubt, strident rows had lost one of the gods of cricket.

Fred's funeral was one of the saddest I have ever attended. I was privileged to be asked by his wife Veronica to attend, along with my co-presenter on *Look North*, Christa Ackroyd. Dickie Bird was to give the eulogy, and I have to say gave one of the finest speeches of his career. From the heart. Fred now rests in Bolton Abbey church-yard. As one of his former fast-bowling partners Mike Cowan commented: "He always had the choice of ends when he bowled". Now, as he overlooks the River Wharfe for ever, he has the best place there too.

12

Dickie Bird

In terms of achievement on the cricket field as a player, Dickie's abilities are modest. His claim to fame for Yorkshire was in making 169 in a county championship match at Park Avenue and then being dropped. That was so in keeping with the way the county was run in those days.

As a young boy playing for Barnsley he played with Michael Parkinson and Geoff Boycott. Parky told me one great tale about Dickie and his pre-match nervousness.

"Dickie was so hyped up before a game that he couldn't stay still. As he waited to go in to bat I saw him chew through his cricket gloves. In those days they were made of horse hair and I swear when he went out to the wicket his mouth was full of it and he had to cough it out."

In another tale Parky told me how "I once saw him buckle his pads together so that when he got up to bat he fell flat on his face".

Dickie was certainly a good player. He recalls, for that same Barnsley team, running out Boycott when the great man was on forty-nine.

"If you reached fifty you got a collection. There was a sizeable crowd there and Boycott was not pleased. 'You have cost me a few quid there,' moaned Boycott. 'Don't worry Geoff,' I said. 'I will share mine with you when I get fifty.' I remember getting about four quid, and I gave Boycs a very generous half-crown. That shows we could be generous in Barnsley."

It is true that Dickie was a misfortune waiting to happen. But the story of him playing for Leicestershire one day beats them all. Fielding at third man, he was wearing rubber-soled shoes. The grass was wet. He raced around to gather up the ball, slipped and, the story goes, found himself between railings with his head stuck in them. Half an hour later a joiner released him from this embarrassing situation.

Dickie's average when he retired in 1964 was just over twenty. He turned to umpiring, thanks to the Middlesex fast bowler John Warr. John spoke to Dickie about what would follow playing cricket.

"I have no idea", said Dickie.

"Well, think about umpiring", replied John.

His new career would turn him into one of the best-known Yorkshiremen of all time. In his twenty years as an umpire he stood in sixty-six Tests. Imagine how many more he would have done these days with Test matches all the year round.

Stories about Dickie have become the stuff of legend but one thing about him is true: he cannot stop worrying about being late.

As I mentioned in the previous chapter he made a stunning tribute to Fred Trueman at his funeral. However, he was so worried about turning up on time that he stayed at the nearby Devonshire Arms the night before. Yet he was still at the church two hours before anyone else.

Indeed, when he attended the baptism of my twin boys Harvey and Harrison in York at an 11.30am service, he

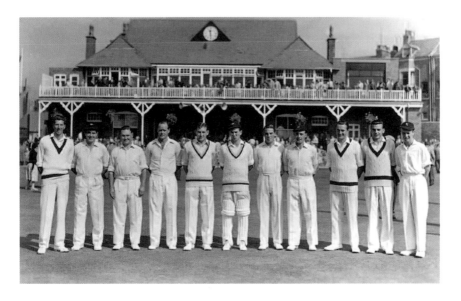

Dickie Bird (second from right) lines up with the Yorkshire team at Scarborough on the 2nd September 1959. The team (including Ken Taylor) had secured the County Championship the previous day at Hove, but Ken had returned to Huddersfield to rejoin his footballing colleagues at Leeds Road. Dickie took Ken's place and in the first innings shared a first-wicket partnership of 146 with Bryan Stott, Dickie scoring fifty-eight. But in the second innings Dickie was bowled by Harold Rhodes for a duck. This match was Dickie's last for Yorkshire.

arrived in time for the 8.30am service as well as the ten o'clock.

"This is costing me a fortune, Harry", he told me. "I've left two collections and now there'll be a third."

One of my favourite stories of Dickie, though, happened in Scarborough and I witnessed the end result. As president of the cricket festival there Dickie took his role very seriously. At times he seemed to want to meet every person who attended it and thank them personally for their support. On the first day, though, Dickie had somehow lost his suitcase on his way there. To this day no one knows where it is but it did contain his dinner suit, shirt and tie. At this stage of his life he was really cock-a-hoop. His book was the bestselling sports biography of all time and he was a millionaire.

Cec Snell, who was chief executive of the festival, advised him to go out and buy a cheap suit to tide him over. We all thought he would head to Debenhams at the top of the town, but no. I saw him scurry into a second-hand store. When he appeared at the ground for his first official function, you have never seen anything like it. The jacket he wore had sleeves so long that a gorilla would have found its arms flapping. The shirt was too big, especially the neck, and his tie was one of those old-fashioned kipper ones. He looked like Austin Powers.

"The whole outfit cost me £5", he said.

Bill Mustoe, one of the festival officials, could hardly conceal his mirth but said, "Dickie, you look like a thousand lira." He then muttered under his breath, "That's about 25p."

But I know of very few people in the cricket world who don't love and respect the man.

He recalls with affection his time as the greatest umpire in the world. He was, as you know, as well-known as any cricketer.

I remember him telling me that the Derbyshire player Ashley Walker once handed him his false teeth on a terrible wicket at Buxton. "If tha don't survive the over", said Dickie, "who shall I give them to?"

In Dickie's last season as an umpire I managed to persuade BBC Sport to let me do a documentary, *Dickie Bird – A Rare Species*, on his final season. It won the Royal

Dickie Bird umpiring his final County Championship match,
Yorkshire v Warwickshire at Headingley in 1998.

Television Society award for best sports documentary and got five million people watching it on BBC 2 — one of the biggest they recorded. I had no trouble in getting people to offer their appreciation of the great man, from Dennis Lillee to Ian Botham.

I suppose it is fair to say that Dickie was the first showman umpire. They are all over the place these days. His mannerisms became part of his legend. Lillee, in one interview I did on another documentary about Dickie, said, "Look at him. A bag of nerves. He twitches all the time. But every Aussie loves him."

Indeed they did, but I wonder what some of the earlier umpiring icons like Sid Buller would have made of him. Not a lot in all probablility.

Dickie was also the first umpire to really take a stand on intimidatory bowling, and he famously no-balled the Lancashire pace bowler Peter Lever ten times when the new front foot rule was introduced.

Dickie's record is a remarkable one but there was one match which I know he often recounts: the Prudential World Cup final in 1975. The match started at 11am and ended in total confusion at 8.45pm. It was a roasting hot day and there was a pitch invasion by thousands of West Indians who thought they had won the World Cup. Sometimes I think we forget the kind of pressures the likes of Dickie were under. For nearly ten hours he and the veteran umpire Tom Spencer had to concentrate like never before. Let's not forget that in the pitch invasion Dickie was actually knocked unconscious.

The greatest accolade came after the match when Clive Lloyd and Ian Chappell both thanked the umpires for their outstanding contributions.

His association with Allan Lamb has been an abiding

memory for Dickie. Allan once gave him a mobile phone in a Test match and of course the set-up resulted in Ian Botham ringing him at the end of an over.

"Dickie Bird here. Test match umpire."

"Ian Botham here, tell Lamby to get a move on."

Allan Lamb was also the culprit who removed all four wheels of Dickie's car at the Oval.

His career record is impressive and I have no doubt that he would have been at the top of his profession had he been umpiring today.

When he went out for his final Test match at Lord's he received a standing ovation. He cried and cried. "I can't believe it's all over. My career, gone in a flash."

Then came his biography, and to this day Dickie can still get a standing ovation wherever he speaks. He is quite simply a smashing bloke.

13
Ellery Hanley

I will always remember a superb piece of television commentary by my old friend Ray French. It was the semi-final of the Rugby League Challenge Cup at Headingley. Bradford Northern (as they were then) were playing Featherstone Rovers. Hanley, then a raw talent, burst down the right from the halfway line.

"Hanley has three players in front of him. One has been brushed away. There goes another. And he's still going. What a try from Ellery Hanley."

I had a love/hate relationship with Hanley. I admired him as a player, but he was a very difficult, prickly person to interview.

This to me was particularly sad. Rugby league has always been the accessible sport. 'No' was not a word used where publicity was concerned. Ellery became what I called the first premiership rugby league player and did himself few favours as a result.

He was unmistakably the greatest player of his generation. His impact was felt not just in England, but also in Australia where he was known as the 'black pearl'.

A West Yorkshire lad, he started playing for amateur side Corpus Christie before he was spotted and snapped up by Bradford Northern. Peter Fox was the coach then and he

Ellery Hanley in his prime, playing for the British Lions against New Zealand in 1985.

once told me that here was the finest athletic talent he had ever seen on a rugby field.

"Ellery had everything", said Peter. "But you always had to be careful how you told him off. He could turn against you in an instant."

He went on the Lions tour to Australia in 1984 and was one of the stars. Indeed, in the following season he had probably his best ever form, scoring over thirty tries. That prompted the next stage of his career and a world record move to Wigan for £150,000.

The club at this time had Maurice Lindsay as chairman and there is no doubt that if anyone could have an influence on Ellery it was Maurice. The proof of that was clear when he scored a staggering sixty-three tries in one season playing in a host of different positions. Here was Ellery's strength. Maurice summed it up to me when I talked to him on *Grandstand's Rugby League Focus*.

"We had an injury crisis one week", said Maurice, "and there are always players who don't want to play out of position no matter what the problem is. Ellery said he would play anywhere for the club and challenged the others to do the same. Strangely, they all did."

But the quiet and difficult side of Ellery was beginning to take over. Countless requests for interview were turned down. He openly ignored many journalists. During this time with the all-conquering Wigan, he became captain of Great Britain and was so close to beating the Aussies on their home turf in 1988.

He impressed the Aussies so much that Balmain signed him and rave reviews followed match after match as he took them to the Australian Grand Final.

He has always been a very shrewd operator and in 1991 he decided that it was time to move away from Central Park. He had won the lot there. Now to the new challenge of Leeds. His fee hit the dizzy rugby league heights of £250,000 and, despite being over thirty, he scored over 100 tries in his Headingley life. One further record came his way at the age of thirty-four: as a forward he scored thirty-four tries.

In all he had 428 tries to his name.

He became coach of Great Britain and St Helens with real distinction and eventually softened his 'no talk' approach. Ironically I had a hand in that. In 1994 I left the BBC for what proved a very poor move for me as the public affairs executive of the Rugby League. Countless press inquiries for an Ellery Hanley interview landed on my desk, day after day. Then one day I took the bull by the horns. I invited some of the top writers to a lunch and persuaded Ellery to come along too. There he displayed eloquence, and a real passion and joy for his role as captain. The resulting articles made Ellery realise that he could use the media to his advantage at times.

I maintain to this day that there is no finer sight in sport than seeing Ellery Hanley lead by example on the pitch. Something he did every time he pulled on a jersey, whether it was Wigan, Leeds or Great Britain. He won the Adidas Golden Boot in 1989 which confirmed his status as an all-time great.

These days he is a more than useful squash player, still incredibly fit and, as seen on television, can ice skate as well.

14
Don Fox

Heroes come in many shapes and sizes. Some are tragic. None more so than Don Fox, brother of the great Neil. It can't have been easy to be compared alongside the god that was Neil. But Don made a pretty good fist of it. The other brother Peter became a great coach with the 'biggest gob in rugby league', so he coped with Neil in his own way.

The sadness of Don, who we lost in August 2008, was that he will be remembered for one thing. The famous 'Watersplash Final' of 1968. The match pitted Wakefield Trinity against Leeds. Everyone expected that this would be the classic final. But a torrential downpour turned it into a farce. In all truth the game should never have been played. But the BBC had devoted all of its *Grandstand* coverage to the game and there would have been a very large hole on the TV screens had it been postponed. To make matters worse, the heavens opened again during the match and it was virtually impossible for players not to fall down once they went over walking pace. Full credit to both teams. They made the match compelling and desperately close.

It's worth recalling how the drama built to its great climax in the last minutes of the game. Seventy-eight

Don Fox practises his kicking at Wakefield Trinity's Belle Vue ground before the 1968 Challenge Cup Final.

minutes on the clock and Bev Risman landed his fourth goal of the final. Leeds led at that stage 11-7. The team's ribbons were minutes away from being placed on the famous trophy. From the kick-off the ball stopped instantly in a mini-lake and Ken Hirst fly-hacked the ball forward. The Leeds defenders couldn't get their footing and Ken managed to dribble over for one of the most sensational tries in the history of the cup. That made the score 11-10 (tries in those days were only worth three points). The goal kick, worth two points, was to follow. It was left to the utterly dependable Don Fox to snatch Wakefield an unlikely victory with the simplest of kicks in front of the posts. He had already been named the Lance Todd Trophy winner for man of the match and had kicked two far more difficult goals earlier.

The BBC commentator was the great Eddie Waring. Many people used to criticise Eddie but I will tell you this: Eddie had a genuine feeling for all the players and his popularity in the south of England was off the scale. His commentary is still regarded as one of the greatest ever on live sport and certainly ranks alongside Ken Wolstenholme's in the 1966 World Cup — you know the one, "They think it's all over … it is now".

Even now Eddie's commentary is astonishing for how it portrayed one man's lapse:

"So the Challenge Cup final depends on this kick. He's missed it. He's missed it. He's a poor lad."

Don held his head in his hands and became the stuff of legend.

One of his team-mates, though, is quick to say that Don should never even have taken that kick. "From time to time we had a system which would look at the angle of the kick and I would take the shot if it was on my side. I

Don Fox attempts the last-minute kick in the 1968 'Watersplash Final' which would have won the Challenge Cup for Wakefield. Don's unfortunate miss and Eddie Waring's commentary have gone down in rugby league folklore.

expected that I might even take this kick. But Don just decided to take it himself."

On the Monday following the final, *Look North* persuaded him to go down to Wakefield Trinity's ground Belle Vue and do the kick again. Without his boots and in his carpet slippers he was successful ten times out of ten.

Don Fox scores a try for Featherstone Rovers in their famous victory over the touring Australians at Post Office Road on 2nd October 1963. Don, who finished with a personal haul of seventeen points, felt that this was the finest match of his career.

"I won the Lance Todd Trophy for my efforts before the kick at Wembley", said Don. "All people remember me for now is missing that bl★★★★y kick."

I think it is fair to say that he was haunted by that miss for the rest of his life. He felt as if he had let his team-mates down, although not one of them even remotely felt that was the case. He was beaten by the freak weather, nothing else.

But we will not forget that as a Featherstone Rovers player he holds the record for most tries scored: 162. He is also third in the all-time goal-kicking lists with 503 in

Don, with his wife Mary, holds the 1967-8 Championship trophy at the civic reception in Wakefield.

369 appearances. He only achieved one cap — in 1963 against the Aussies as loose forward. He teamed up with brother Neil, who was responsible for getting him on the books at Wakefield in 1965. His transfer fee was £3,500 and they enjoyed a rich few years together.

But he always retained a loyalty to his roots in the mining industry. At the age of fifteen he left school and joined Sharlston Colliery as a joiner. Thirty-five years later he was there again when the pit closed.

For me Don will always go down as one of rugby league's greats.

15
Willie Watson

I never saw Willie play either soccer or cricket when he was in his pomp. But I did share, through my closest friend at school, Graham, a close connection with him.

Graham was Willie's son and we were inseparable at St Peter's in York because of our love of all sports. Graham left for Johannesberg in 1968 when his dad was made chief coach of the Wanderers club. In the years before we went on holidays together and our two families became pretty close. For my father Morris it was the greatest thrill of his life. Willie was his sporting hero. Graham and I were both in the first XI at school when the MCC brought its team to face us. Fred Trueman was there and so too was Willie Watson. He proceeded to give us a master class of batsmanship, making fifty-seven effortlessly and then giving his son his wicket by dollying up a catch to mid-off.

His home in Huddersfield was a regular venue for my summer holidays, and on one occasion he took me to Paddock Cricket Club where his love of the game really matured. As a fourteen-year-old he hit 122 in a cup tie against Lascelles Hall. Strangely, when Yorkshire started to notice him he made a spectacularly unsuccessful start: a duck for Yorkshire seconds, followed by two and another duck. Then he made sixty against Lancashire.

*Willie Watson (right) and Brian Close walk to the wicket at
North Marine Road, Scarborough, for Yorkshire v MCC in 1954.*

In the middle of all of this he was making a name for himself at Huddersfield Town. The war took him into the army where his talents were soon recognised. He played alongside Tommy Lawton, Matt Busby, Tom Finney and Joe Mercer.

After the war Willie was in demand as a footballer and cricketer. Yorkshire clearly saw him as vital to their 1946 rebuilding plans. He spent a few seasons opening the batting alongside the great Len Hutton, before dropping to his favoured position down the order.

How anyone could cope with the pressure of two sports at that level I will never know. In the end I suppose in his soccer days he took the main battering and he became player-manager of Halifax Town. In cricket he was always under pressure and eventually lost his England place in 1954.

Willie of course holds one very special distinction. In 1953 he filled the front page of the *Daily Sketch* newspaper. The headline quite simply said "Wonderful Willie Watson". Some say that Willie's defiance against the Aussies on this day is one to rival any in sport. It is important to set the scene. Good old *Test Match Special* was listened to by the whole nation as England tried to save the Lord's Test match. The facts speak for themselves. At the close of the fourth day England were 20-3 chasing a target of over 340 to win in seven hours. The fourth wicket pair dug in and batted doggedly to move the score to seventy-three before Denis Compton was run out. This is where thousands of English cricket supporters tuned into the BBC for coverage of history unfolding. At lunch England had moved on to 116-4. By tea time the scoreboard clocked up 183-4. Trevor Bailey, one of the great stayers at the crease, made his fifty in three-and-half

Willie Watson (front row, second from left) in the Yorkshire team which played Middlesex at Lord's in 1954. This photograph includes six of my Yorkshire Sporting Heroes: Watson, Fred Trueman (back row, left), Bob Appleyard, Ray Illingworth and Brian Close (back row, third, second and first right), and Len Hutton (front row, second from right).

hours. Together they put on 163 for the fifth wicket. Willie, in true Boycott style, hung on for just short of six hours for his 109. But that wasn't the end of the drama. Willie's account sums it all up: "I was caught at slip with forty minutes left. I undressed and had a bath then I heard another great roar. Trevor was out. For a moment I thought, surely we can't lose the match now."

Fortunately Freddie Brown and Godfrey Evans batted out the rest of the game and England finished on 282-7. In the following matches the Aussies were only thirty short of a victory at Leeds and in the final Test England beat the Aussies to win the Ashes.

Willie left Yorkshire for Leicestershire in 1957 and was an outstanding success. He headed the averages with over 2,000 runs in 1959 and eventually became assistant secretary and captain of the county. As mentioned, he left for South Africa in 1968 to coach at the Wanderers club.

I talked for hours with Willie. Cricket was his main love but he was also a wonderful soccer player. He never achieved the adulation of Denis Compton but is one of those rare double internationals who have graced sport.

He was also the most modest sports star I have ever met. He underplayed his achievements and he completely ran away from the spotlight. These days that could not happen. Both sports are twelve-month commitments, but let no one take anything away from what Willie achieved.

Surprisingly his statistics hardly tell the real story of what a quality player he was. In the first-class game he scored 25,670 runs for an average of 39.9. He played twenty-three Tests for an average of only 25.85.

My great friend Dickie Bird remembered Willie at Leicestershire and to this day says that he was one of the very best batsmen he had ever seen on a dodgy wicket.

16
Michael Vaughan

The Yorkshire cricket born-and-bred policy is something I have passionately believed in for most of my life. But so too was the belief that Yorkshire would always be a force in cricket. When the latter became a distant memory, the former gave way to realism.

Leaving aside overseas cricketers who became exceptions to the Yorkshire-only policy, the county did find itself embarrassed back in 1906 when one Cec Parkin was found out. He had been born in Durham and was summarily dispatched to Lancashire immediately the dastardly deed had been discovered.

So to the curious case of Michael Vaughan. Born in Eccles, he moved to Yorkshire at the age of nine. The diehards (and in the past I would have been one of them) put up strong opposition when this became public. But wisely the committee decided that here was a rich talent we could not lose.

I have often wondered if the fact that he learned his game in the Yorkshire camp helped him develop into the outstanding captain of England that he became. In all the furore of events in August 2008 when, after losing a Test series against South Africa, he resigned the captaincy, we often forget what a brilliant leader he was on the field as a batsman. Take 2000-1, for example, when he was ranked as the best batsman in the world.

He also joined one of the most exclusive clubs in Yorkshire sporting history when, alongside F S Jackson, Sir Len Hutton and Ray Illingworth, be became the latest tyke to win the Ashes.

Martyn Moxon presents a youthful Michael Vaughan with his Yorkshire cap at Scarborough in 1995.

I have always found Michael to be a thoroughly decent lad. I played a round of golf with him in 2002 and he explained to me his philosophy of leadership:

"I want all the players to trust me and know that I will always back them up as long as they show the team and me the same loyalty."

I think that explains why so many of the players, notably Kevin Pieterson, backed him when Michael resigned the captaincy in 2008. He brought the best out of all the players during the 2005 Ashes series, notably Matthew Hoggard. Under Vaughan's guidance, Hoggard became the fifth best seam bowler in the world and he took so many crucial wickets in that series just when his captain needed them.

He was bedevilled by a knee injury which threatened his career but he refused to give in. He went to Wayne Morton, the former Yorkshire and England physio, for treatment and greatly impressed Wayne: "He is one of the most determined men I have ever treated. A true Yorkie — even if he is a Lancastrian."

The sad aspect of being an international cricketer these days is that your county rarely gets to see you in action. I have always believed this to be wrong. But make no mistake about Michael, he cares deeply about the county. His record, therefore, will not look overly impressive. But let's not forget that he made a century on his debut against, of all teams, the county of his birth, Lancashire. He rattled up three more centuries in his first season and a new star was born.

His outstanding achievement was in leading England to glory in what was surely the most dramatic Ashes series in the modern age. I am the first to acknowledge the achievements of Ray Illingworth and Sir Len Hutton, but

Vaughan's success came under the most intense public and television scrutiny the game has ever known.

The build-up to the 2005 Ashes was something to behold. Vaughan immediately stamped his mark on the series when his opposite number, Ricky Ponting, called for a catching pact. He wanted Vaughan to accept the word of fielders rather than the umpire. Michael preferred the umpire's word. England were trounced in the first Test and there were those who were beginning to question whether Vaughan's form was being affected because of his role as skipper. It wasn't until the third Test that he silenced the critics, albeit with a huge slice of luck. He was dropped on forty-one and then clean bowled by a 'McGrath special' the next ball. Fortunately it was a no-ball and Vaughan went on to make 166. The rest, as they say, is history.

He was given the OBE for his achievement and the freedom of the city of Sheffield followed. There was also that never-to-be-forgotten parade through London when cricket, for once, matched football for newspaper headlines and television coverage.

Like any entrepreneur he managed to rattle off a book to coincide with the end of the series. I met up with him at a book signing in Sheffield and have never seen a hangover like it.

Sport, though, can be so cruel and I feel it has been to Michael Vaughan. After winning the Ashes he desperately wanted to defend it in Australia. They say this is the ultimate test of a captain. But that nagging knee problem developed into a serious one and at that stage his career was very much on the line. He missed the 2007 tour of Australia, watching it from the sidelines, and England were given the beating of their lives.

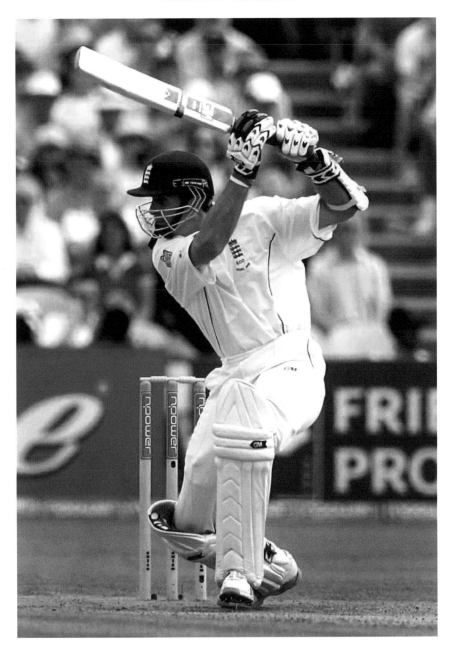

*Michael Vaughan drives his way to a half-century during the third
Ashes Test against Australia at Old Trafford in 2005.*

Michael Vaughan joined a select group of English cricket captains when his team regained the Ashes from the Australians at the end of a titanic Test series in 2005.

Would it have been different had he captained the side? Well the facts are that he seemed to raise his game when the Aussies were the opposition, so I believe he would have had a very significant impact. Remember he made 633 runs against them in 2002-3 including three centuries.

In a total of eighty-two Tests against all opposition he scored 5,719 runs including eighteen centuries with an average of 41.44.

Michael announced his retirement from Yorkshire and first-class cricket in June 2009, having scored 16,295 runs including forty-two centuries with an average of 36.95. His retirement was a sad way to end his career. I'm not sure it was handled as well as it could have been by the cricket authorities.

His statistics as our national captain will stand the test of time with anyone. He led England fifty-one times and won twenty-six, and no one doubted that Vaughan was a formidable adversary on the field.

So just how good a captain was Michael?

"In the dressing room he commanded total respect and his authority was never questioned." (Dickie Bird)

"I believe he prospered from the Yorkshire upbringing that is part of the game. We always know a good skipper and he was one." (Fred Trueman)

"He led by example on the pitch. Tactically he was very sound and got the best out of all his players when it mattered the most." (Geoff Boycott)

17
Chris Waddle

When Billy Bremner was manager of Doncaster Rovers we met up for a sporting dinner and, long after everyone had gone, Billy and I ended up in his office at the ground. We talked about current players he would have wanted in his team.

"Without a doubt the best passer of a ball I have seen is Chris Waddle", Billy told me. "This lad could have been the greatest midfielder of all time. He isn't bad now."

Praise indeed from the wee man.

To be fair, Billy wasn't the only one who admired him. Michel Platini the great French player said that he would have loved to have had him in the French side: "He was made for the French team."

Waddle recalled how he learned the game in Newcastle: "When I was seven all I wanted to do was play soccer. After school at night we'd play forty a side at times. That is where I learned how to dribble. You had to, otherwise you'd never get a kick of the ball all night."

If you ask any Sheffield Wednesday supporter they will tell you that there was no finer sight for an Owl than watching Waddle at his best. He only played 109 games for Wednesday, and during the 1993 season he won the Football Writers Association Footballer of the Year award.

*There was no more exhilarating sight for a Sheffield Wednesday
fan than Chris Waddle in full flight.*

Chris Waddle, an Owls legend.

He established himself as a regular England player at Tottenham Hotspur and was in the team that reached the World Cup finals in 1986 in Mexico. I went to that World Cup for BBC Sport and well remember his face as he trudged from the pitch after England's defeat.

His move to the French side Olympique de Marseille for a fee of £4.5 million put him alongside a team of stars. Here he was called 'Magic Chris' because of his dribbling skills and trademark free kicks.

His return to Wednesday was prompted by Trevor Francis and the then chairman of the club Dave Richards. Dave has become a much-maligned figure at Hillsborough despite his position as one of the game's supremos, but I can tell you that he was singularly responsible for the bid of £1.25 million which secured Waddle's signing. Under Francis, Wednesday played some great football and the 1992-3 season saw the Owls reach both domestic cup finals.

I witnessed probably the most exhilarating moment in my career while on the way to the FA Cup final. Dave invited me with camera to travel to the stadium in the team coach. I was just in front of Waddle on the bus and saw how he coped with the frenzy of the fans outside. He was listening to some music on his headphones, and serenely smiled and waved as the twin towers approached, and Wednesday's fans went wild. Wednesday lost both those finals although Chris did score in the replay.

At this time I was working every week for *Match of the Day*. Alan Hansen, who is still the best analyst in the game as far as I am concerned, praised Waddle week after week. This led to one of the mysteries of the modern game. He was head and shoulders above everyone in midfield, and yet England manager Graham Taylor ignored him.

Many people these days think that the 'step-over' was perfected by Ronaldo while at Manchester United. They should have seen Waddle. Originally a left winger, he played some of the best football of his career on the right, and that trick deceived countless fullbacks to allow a rampant David Hirst to score a stack of goals for Wednesday. Mark Bright picked up a few as well in an Owls team that had a lot of flair.

Sadly injuries affected his later years at Hillsborough and once again he found he was frozen out by a manager, this time David Pleat.

These days Waddle is in rich demand as a pundit on all the major channels. He openly admits that his favourite footballers are the ones who were in many ways like him: Rodney Marsh, Stan Bowles and Frank Worthington.

"When I watch a game I'm looking for someone who breaks the mould", says Chris. "A bit like a thief unpicking a lock. There are few who can."

One footnote on Waddle's Yorkshire connection came at Bradford City after signing for them in 1996. His fabulous goal in the FA Cup in February 1997 against Everton is still talked about at Valley Parade.

18
Norman Hunter

When you meet Norman Hunter he is far from the fearsome competitor that terrorised many forwards during the Leeds United glory years. Outside of Leeds he was just a 'dirty' player. His style of play summed up why people hated the way Leeds played. Unashamedly one-footed, many experts on the game belittled his skill. But he could play.

His worse moment came in 1974. England were up against Poland in that must-win match for England to qualify for the World Cup in West Germany. I can see it now: failing in the kind of tackle he never missed in all his years at Leeds. It led to Poland scoring and he admitted years later just how much it affected him:

"I am a tough character but all the newspaper reports made it clear that I had cost England their place in the World Cup. It was true I had. But I did mark down the names of those journalists who were particularly vindictive about me."

Norman's nickname was 'Bites Yer Legs', and loads of football followers will remember with horror and relish the on-pitch fight he had with Francis Lee of Derby County in November 1975.

Let's be fair: Leeds United's defence was fearsome. Jack

Norman Hunter was nicknamed 'Bites Yer Legs' for a good reason.

Charlton was as tough as they come and with Norman alongside him no team fancied playing against them.

At the same time of course, there was another hard man who would claim to be the toughest of them all, Tommy Smith of Liverpool. In all the games they played against each other I don't think they ever clashed.

Norman's sixteen years at Leeds brought him just about all the honours the game could give: championships, cup winner's medals and, in 1974, the first ever PFA Player of the Year award. For Norman that meant so much. It was an acknowledgement that, while he was the game's hard man, he could also play.

His record of consistency is remarkable. The worst season he had for appearances was 1974-5 when he played only twenty-five league games. Prior to that he was well into the forties most seasons and only dipped when he was serving a suspension or two. He scored a few goals with that left foot — eighteen in all — in a career which saw him clock up 540 games in the league for Leeds, and another 184 in other competitions.

The recent publication of the book on Brian Clough and the film *The Damned United* have led to new stories of Norman and what happened in Clough's forty-four days at Elland Road. It is said that in one practice match in which Cloughie played, Norman allowed his frustrations to show when he chopped the manager down with one of his trademark tackles. "Welcome to Leeds, Mr Clough", said one of the squad.

He left Leeds in 1976 as part of a mass clearout after that devastating loss in the European Cup final in Paris. Bristol City tempted him and it's interesting how the fans at Ashton Gate reacted to his arrival and departure. At first they really didn't want this 'dirty so-and-so' as part of their set-up. That changed very quickly. He spent three years there and was soon the fans' favourite. He kept them in the old First Division during those years and when he left they were promptly relegated.

It's funny, isn't it, when you look at ex-players and have to predict how they would fare as managers, surely Norman would have been right up there? But no. He was a player-manager at Barnsley and also took over at Rotherham. He even returned to Elland Road but left when Howard Wilkinson became manager.

19

Darren Gough

When Darren first burst onto the scene I was asked by *Sportsnight*, the BBC's midweek flagship programme, to do a feature on him. They wanted me to give a Yorkshireman's view of the new kid on the block. He was so refreshing to deal with. Anything we wanted he would give us. I loved his commitment to Yorkshire. It was a hard school to follow, including Fred Trueman to name but one. In truth, though, you wouldn't want to mention Fred's name to Darren towards the end of his career. They did not like each other. How typical is that in the story of Yorkshire cricket?

But Gough's talent was there for all to see. He had a lovely action, so different from Trueman's but no less effective. His is a leaping sideways-on action which those in the know call 'skiddy'. I think this made him able to swing the ball very late and he had one delivery I would have died for — the inswinging yorker.

Darren was born in Monk Bretton, the same village near Barnsley that produced Martyn Moxon. He had football trials with Rotherham United where he was described as an aggressive midfielder but opted in the end for cricket where he was nurtured by one of the best coaches of fast bowling in the country, Steve Oldham.

Darren Gough bowling for England. Darren earned the respect of the Aussies for his wholehearted approach to the game.

England's Darren Gough bowls past umpire Daryll Hair during the Test match against Pakistan at Lord's in 2001.

His obvious enjoyment in playing for Yorkshire and England was infectious — more so than most players I know. He always had a smile on him and that made him incredibly popular in Yorkshire. Indeed, I would go so far as to say that, in his pomp, he was alongside Boycott in the popularity stakes.

This was confirmed in a massive way when he won *Strictly Come Dancing.* You may remember that he had asked for the winter off and would therefore miss the tour of Pakistan which very few cricketers enjoy. He then popped up on the BBC programme and in typical fashion trained like mad to become a truly outstanding dancer. I think he won that award because of his army of Yorkshire fans. I went to a cricket society meeting a few days before the final of the competition and the 100 people who were there all said they would be voting for him at least five times. The 'Dazzler' was greatly admired.

The Australians loved Darren as well. The way he played his cricket was like the way they played: total effort and commitment.

Two matches must stand out in his career. In 1994-5 on the tour to Australia, in the third Test he hit a cavalier fifty-one and then produced some hostile bowling that reaped him six wickets for only forty-nine runs. The Aussies only just managed a draw. He was given a standing ovation by the Aussies on that day, and was awarded player of the match.

The second was his hat-trick against the Aussies in 1999. Now that is a very exclusive club. It was fitting that Goughie's last ever wicket was that of Aussie Darren Langer who was playing for Somerset.

Marcus Trescothick, the England opening batsman, is one who has a deep respect for Gough. In his autobiography he says Darren's achievements are outstanding:

"The great thing about Darren is that he is such an instinctive bowler. He could adapt quickly to situations and you know he would give you everything every time he pulled on that England sweater. He also always gave you the impression that he was loving every minute of it. Something our fast bowlers have forgotten, I think."

The one thing that Darren gave to cricket was an injection of personality. It is not something which flows richly in the game. He became genuinely loved because of his smile and effusive character. That made him so different not only to Fred Trueman, but also the current moody breed of players. They could all learn a lesson or two from him. As David Lloyd the commentator and former England player said:

"Just watch the reception that Gough receives when he is not bowling. If he is fielding at third man or wherever in the outfield, he is bantering with the crowd all the time. That is what cricket is all about. It is what the Dazzler is all about too."

He retired as England's all time wicket taker for one-day internationals with 234, and his fifty-eight Test matches brought an impressive haul of 229 wickets.

His testimonial in Yorkshire was an outstanding success. Then, much to many people's surprise, he left the county to join Essex. He had played fifteen years for Yorkshire but he returned in a wave of emotion in 2007. The county needed Darren to reinvigorate the dressing room and he got off to a flier as well with three wins in the first few matches.

I think it would be fair to say that when he retired at the end of the 2008 season, the club had really failed to latch on to Darren's legacy. They avoided relegation without him at Hove, but he clearly left a united team behind him.

I think he wanted to retire a few years before he eventually did at the age of thirty-eight. But on his return to Yorkshire we had him as our guest on *Look North* and he was overwhelmed by the reaction of the Yorkshire cricket club members. "I had forgotten just what cricket means to this county", he said. He soon remembered, though, what the county thought of him.

20

Bob Appleyard

If ever there was a cricketer who was underrated, that man must be Bob Appleyard. In recent years he graced Yorkshire County Cricket Club as its president, and did so with style and dignity. His love of Bradford and Park Avenue in particular was a main passion in his life.

His was a ridiculously short career. He didn't start until the age of twenty-seven.

I have often asked him how he described his style of bowling. "I was a fast off-spinner", he replied.

Bryan Stott the former Yorkshire opening batsman told me that he was unique because of his dipping flight and unerring accuracy. "Put him on a wet wicket and he was totally unplayable", he told me.

He was also a kind of precursor to one Geoff Boycott for practising. Apparently he would spend hours in the nets bowling at one stump when all the other players had long gone in for a bath. He was greatly encouraged by Norman Yardley who wanted him to develop an off-break. He worked on it to such an extent that he could bowl it at full pace with no detrimental effect.

But his personal life was dogged by the kind of problems with which few of us would ever be able to cope. When he was seven his mother left home. At thirteen he lost his younger sister Margaret to diphtheria, and at fifteen his father, stepmother and two little sisters were found gassed in the bathroom of their home. Fortunately the parents of his stepmother took Bob into their home and as devout Christians they cared for him in a strict upbringing. Far from turning away from religion, Bob became heavily involved in it and his faith, I am sure, helped him cope with the challenges that were still ahead. For many of us, what he had suffered so far would be bad enough, but more was to follow.

The war years put a halt to his cricketing career but after the conflict he went for nets in the Bradford League with Bowling Old Lane Cricket Club. He was spotted immediately by the club president Ernest Holdsworth. I spoke to Bob about his Yorkshire debut back in 1950.

"Hardly spectacular", he told me. "I seem to recall taking eleven wickets in three matches. But then came 1951."

This was Bob's first campaign proper and he took a staggering 200 wickets, the first time ever a player had done this in his first season. In his excellent book about Bob, Stephen Chalke talks of the wonderful versatility of his bowling. He could be quick or bowl off-spin but he also could deliver leg-cutters or off-cutters, with devastating accuracy.

After all he had gone through, surely a kind God would have allowed this to be the spur for a career at the very top? No way. In the middle of his momentous season he fell ill for a short time and was diagnosed with pleurisy. But at the start of the next season the true extent of his illness became apparent: tuberculosis. It was so unfair. He was actually at death's door for quite some time and the thought of a return to cricket was inconceivable.

This man, though, is quite simply the very definition of

Bob Appleyard photographed in August 1950. For me, Bob is the very definition of a Yorkshireman for the way he has faced up to the many adversities in his life.

I once asked Bob Appleyard to describe his bowling style:
"I was a fast off-spinner", he told me.

a Yorkshireman. He refused to give in and next season he was back in the county team and taking 154 wickets.

An England call-up seemed so richly deserved, and no one begrudged him 5-51 on his debut and in a nine Test match run a thirty-one wicket haul. His tour to Australia in 1954 was surely one of the highlights of his troubled career.

Sadly he was effectively forced out of the game with a chronic shoulder injury and, after five short years, he retired. Imagine what he could have achieved with more luck.

But that is by no means the end of the story of this man. Cricket still occupied his life but so too did one of the biggest con men and crooks this country has ever known, Robert Maxwell. Bob worked for the British Printing Corporation in 1981 when it was taken over by Maxwell. It didn't take him long to take on Maxwell and when the disgraced tycoon sacked Bob that was far from the end of it. Indeed, Bob fought him tooth and nail, won his case and wisely took his pension out of the Maxwell company.

Of all the people I have met in sport, Bob will go down as the unluckiest, and yet he has never displayed a hint of bitterness which most people would have done. His Christian faith clearly helped even when he was again battered with the loss of his young son from leukaemia and later his grandson too.

In later years he championed a cause close to my heart — fighting to bring back cricket to Bradford Park Avenue. The Yorkshire Academy was established on the ground and, with support from Brian Close and Ray Illingworth, it looked as if some form of regular cricket would return.

I have no hesitation in singling out Bob as one of the genuine heroes not just of sport but in Yorkshire history.

21

John Spencer

In the early days of Radio Leeds our radio car helped us provide live broadcasts for our flagship sports programme on a Saturday afternoon. This was well before the days of football commentary which is the staple diet now of every sports broadcast. Rugby was always the cornerstone of our afternoon, either league or union. We were regular visitors to Headingley which in the early 1970s was the top union club in the county, although Morley certainly went close on a number of occasions.

The sports editor John Helm sent one of our top commentators Tim Heley to cover one particular game. Now Tim was a league man really but had a lovely turn of phrase and could turn his hand to anything. The match was Headingley against Nottingham and of course John Spencer was playing. The radio car arrived late because of a technical problem. Tim was flustered but began commentary as soon as he could and described a wonderful try from John as he weaved his way through three defenders to score under the posts: "So Headingley lead early on thanks to Spencer's great try. Back to the studio." A few minutes later we handed back to Tim where he had to apologise: "Sorry about this but Headingley are not playing in their traditional colours. So it's Nottingham who lead."

John Spencer leads out Cambridge University as captain against Harlequins at Twickenham in December 1969.

John Spencer (left) with his England centre partner
David Duckham.

John was upset after the match that he hadn't been credited with the try!

John was a wonderful rugby union player. He learned his trade whilst at Sedbergh School and went on to play in three Varsity matches between 1967-9.

He became the stalwart of Headingley Rugby Union, a club which amalgamated with city rivals Kirkstall before the cross-code merger with the Leeds Rhinos rugby league club. Headingley played next to the River Aire and we always lamented why this club couldn't go one stage further and become a big club like Bath or Leicester.

John was always regarded as a classy centre capable of a turn of pace which would leave his opponents clutching at thin air.

John played fourteen times for England, making his international debut against Ireland at Lansdowne Road. Fourteen caps doesn't sound much but of course there are so many more union internationals played these days. He went on to captain England on four occasions and also went on the Lions tour to New Zealand in 1971.

But whilst his accomplishments on the field are significant, I think another part of John's pedigree is what he

John Spencer, with the ball, on his way to scoring a try for England against Scotland at Murrayfield in 1970.

*During the 1971 British Lions tour to New Zealand,
John Spencer (right) was instructed to train with
the Lions forwards. After forty practice scrums with
Willie John McBride (left), this was the result.*

John Spencer (third row on left) in the British Lions squad which toured New Zealand in 1971.

has given to the game since he retired. He is now one of the most respected names in the game at Rugby Football Union headquarters and constantly gives his all to promoting the success of England's team. For all that commitment and involvement he still maintains an association with the Dales and Grassington in particular where he was born. He loves Wharfedale Rugby Union club where he is president, and for me the hallmark of a sporting great is what they put back into the sport they loved.

I have heard John speak many times on the after-dinner circuit where his skills are still very evident. I once asked him what was the greatest try he ever scored. A momentary pause brought this response:

"No doubt about that. The one Tim Heley described on Radio Leeds all those years ago."

22
David Bairstow

If anyone embodied the spirit of Yorkshire it was David Bairstow. When I was at school I went for trials at Yorkshire. 'Bluey' had just been called up to play for the county while he was doing his A-Levels. I was actually at Headingley the morning the drama unfolded. He arrived at the ground just after 10am having been allowed to sit his English Literature exam at 7am. Even then he looked the part. He was also following in the footsteps of the great Jimmy Binks who'd been the Yorkshire keeper during that fantastic success in the 1960s. David took this chance magnificently and for the next twenty years he was in the team almost without exception.

A young David Bairstow, wearing his 2nd XI sweater, playing at North Marine Road, Scarborough.

Phil Carrick often talked about the role David had in the Yorkshire team during what was a very lean time for the club, certainly as far as championship success was concerned. "He was not a great wicketkeeper", said Phil. "Nor was he a great batsman. But I will tell you this, he was a great cricketer." I suppose that may sound double dutch, but to those who saw his commitment to the county in the leanest of times, it was very clear.

I have often talked about how statistics sometimes cloud reality. His 961 dismissals put him in the top six of all wicketkeepers, although the number of stumpings, 138, may suggest that technically he was flawed. Indeed, he was known at times as 'iron hands'. But you need to appreciate the real strength of David to understand why he is still held in such affection today by Yorkshire members. He never thought there was a lost cause. He talked all the time behind the stumps, urging his team-mates on. If you watched him in the field, he always ran at the end of an over and was first to be ready for the next over.

As a one-day cricketer he was at his most effective. He intimidated the bowling by sheer aggression. One innings in particular sums up why for me David will always be at the top of my admiration. I was working as sports editor for Radio Leeds at the time. It was 1981 and a Benson and Hedges cup tie against Derbyshire at Derby. Yorkshire were nine men down and facing an exit from the competition. To make matters worse, David was joined by a debutant, Mark Johnson. Bluey hit nine sixes. He talked to Johnson virtually every ball and you knew what he was saying: "Just stay there and I will win it". Yorkshire won the game with Bairstow 103 and Johnson not out 4.

He only played four Test matches for England with a batting average of just over twenty, a victim of being

David Bairstow with the 1983 John Player League Trophy.

number two to Bob Taylor. In 1979 he went on the India tour where he made fifty-nine — his highest score in his short international career.

However, his one-day cricket career was significant. He found himself on the first tour of Australia after the Packer fiasco, and featured in one great win at Sydney. He was joined at the wicket by another great Yorkshire character, Graham Stevenson, needing thirty-five to win from six overs. "We'll piss this", he said. Remarkably they did.

He found himself in the middle of the Yorkshire 'civil war' during the Boycott controversy. He always kept his counsel on the issue but I know he had a strong friendship with Boycott which was maintained over many years.

But taking over as captain of the county was far from easy. Yet he achieved cult status within the critical mass of Yorkshire's embittered supporters. They loved him and gave him total support, even if some of the years were acutely disappointing for all to bear. He took over with Yorkshire bottom of the championship and there were slight improvements year on year. The attack was weak; Yorkshire's born-and-bred policy was ruthlessly exposed as other counties fielded world-class overseas players. People forget this. It was still eleven true Yorkies on display against unfair odds.

There is no doubt that the captaincy affected him. His form deteriorated. He played with injuries that should have kept him out for weeks. The pressure for success was increasing. When he lost the captaincy it hurt him as much as it did to Boycott. I did an interview with him on *Look North* which I never broadcast because his emotions just overflowed. He was also under pressure to relinquish the gloves in favour of Steve Rhodes. He refused in typical manner and Rhodes left for Worcestershire.

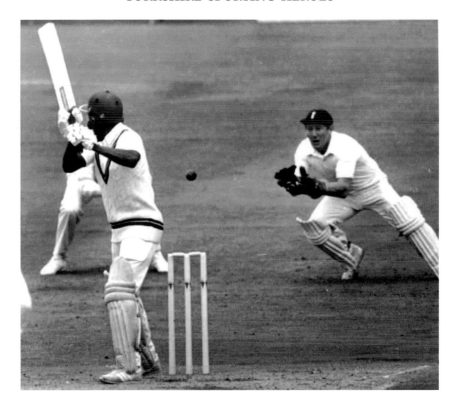

David Bairstow takes another diving catch for Yorkshire.

His suicide in 1998 was greeted by the whole cricket world with genuine sadness and disbelief. I know he had some money problems but he couldn't come to terms with a life after cricket. He'd been enmeshed in the county since he was seventeen years of age.

The legacy, however, is continuing, and what a prospect his young son Johnny could be. Boycott himself has said: "Johnny is a better wicketkeeper, a better batsman, and he will keep the name Bairstow alive in Yorkshire."

I can think of no finer memorial to a Yorkshire Sporting Hero.

23
Roger Millward

One of the best times the game of rugby league has enjoyed surely must be when Hull FC and Hull Kingston Rovers were vying for top honours. Hull is mad about the sport, and no one is held in higher regard than Roger Millward.

Roger is one of the finest players ever to have played for Hull KR. He was club captain at the age of twenty-one and a regular in the international team.

In an era when everyone says that size matters, where on earth do you place 'Roger the Dodger' in that category? He was five feet four inches, weighed just ten stone, and yet was living proof that if you are good enough it doesn't matter if you are, to use a good Yorkshire phrase, 'a titch'.

Success was hard to achieve for Rovers. But in 1978-9, after a fifty-year wait, they won the Division One championship. But it was the following year when the legend of Roger the Dodger was born. The Challenge Cup final that year was Hull FC v Hull KR. At the time I was the Radio 2 rugby league correspondent and can well remember the fanaticism of that weekend.

I worked on a documentary which we called *The Day Hull Closed*. Simple really. Most of the city headed to Wembley and shops decided that it would be better to have a day off than compete with the biggest event in the city's sporting history.

I went with Roger and the team to the stadium on the traditional day before the final. Roger was strangely quiet and clearly becoming focused.

"It suddenly hit me what was at stake", said Roger. "But do you know the time my nerves jangled was actually some ninety minutes before the match started. We went out in our suits and I swear that 30,000 Robins fans were already in the ground. They made such a noise. We had to win it for them."

The game, though, will be etched in my memory for the bravery of Roger, who broke his jaw after just twenty minutes and yet played the entire match.

"As soon as I made the tackle I knew the jaw was broken. Then a few minutes later I made another tackle on Steve 'Knocker' Norton and my jaw caught his knee, and I could feel and hear the jaw click back into place. I remember saying to him after that, 'Thanks mate, you have just lost the game now'."

Rovers of course beat Hull in that game 10-5. Some 95,000 fans saw the game. That Rovers team was a really talented outfit. Phil Lowe, Brian Lockwood and Len Casey gave the side real experience in the pack.

"We'd worked on a routine in training that we thought would open up Hull's defence", Roger explained. "We must have tried it twenty-six times and not once did it work. Anyway we tried it in the final. And lo and behold we scored a try. It was simple really, involving Agar and Holdstock, with Phil Lockwood delaying the third pass. He did it to perfection and Steve Hubbard went over in the corner. None of us could really believe it had worked."

Len Casey told me many years ago that Roger's bravery

A proud day for Roger Millward as his Hull KR team beat arch-rivals Hull 10-5 in the 1980 Challenge Cup Final.

that day matched anything he had ever seen: "It also tells you something about what beating Hull meant to all of us. We'd all been trying to get away from the frenzy of the build-up and it proved almost impossible. We would all have died on that day to play."

I can still see Roger's smile when he accepted the trophy from the Queen at the end of the game, even if it was agonising for him.

"Strangely at that time I felt no pain at all. But I can remember that when I smiled I looked like that fixed grin of Eric Morecambe."

When the team returned to Hull the next day there was a civic reception and a parade through the city. One half of the great place was strangely quiet. They also formed an elite club at Craven Park called the 10-5 club, a name which lives on today.

Another match stands out for Roger and this was at the very start of his career. In 1967 Hull KR played the touring Australians at Craven Park. It was packed and Roger the Dodger got a hat-trick in a memorable 27-15 win. He scored three tries in a game a further eight times for the Robins and once for Britain on the 1970 tour.

They do say that a player gains more from his fellow professionals in terms of honours than anyone else. That must apply to Roger.

To gain the admiration of Aussies just about says it all. He played for Cronulla Sharks in 1976, and in all had six visits to Australia during the 1970s. His coach then was John Raper.

"What a contribution he made to us in '76", said John. "He played fourteen games for us and his experience gave us real dimension. We beat the top three teams thanks to him."

Roger (right) playing for Great Britain against Australia in 1978. Roger also played club rugby in Australia and was greatly admired by the Aussies.

Roger played forty-seven times on the international scene and he scored twenty tries. For his beloved Hull KR he played 406 times with an impressive 207 tries.

He moved on to coach the Robins in the 1980s and '90s, and his record was impressive. The year 1983-4 was surely the hallmark of his success. Rovers won the league championship and divisional premiership, the first team to do the double. The following year they won the John Player Trophy and the championship, and were only denied in the final of the Yorkshire Cup by arch-rivals Hull.

In all the years I covered rugby league for Radio 2, *Grandstand* and *Look North*, he never refused an interview, win, lose or draw. A decent man and a credit to the game.

135

24

Garry Schofield

G arry has recently been something of a controversial character, but I always marvelled at the number of times his critical predictions came true.

I got to know him well when he became the *Super League Show*'s number one pundit. He always called it as he saw it. He predicted that the Great Britain team would be embarrassed by the Aussies in the World Cup in 2002. They were. We took calls of complaint from Maurice Lindsay, the chief executive of the Rugby Football League, who wanted him removed. But he struck a chord at this time with the fans. They loved his no-nonsense approach and honesty, although he had his detractors too. Many thought he was just negative and his riling of referees was at times a little too close to the knuckle.

He was a superb player, his professional career beginning with Hull back in 1983. A surprise, really, as he had been born in Leeds and rarely did a player of his potential fall through the Leeds RLFC net.

It took him only a year to become a full British Lion, making his debut in Australia. A year after that he wrote himself a place in the record books when he scored four tries in a Test match against New Zealand at Central Park. The Aussies, of course, had noticed this precocious

Garry Schofield's reading of the game was second to none.

talent and offered him the chance to play for the Balmain Tigers in 1986. He was an outstanding success and ended the season as top scorer.

The Aussies used to say all kinds of things to him during games. I suppose the term these days is 'sledging'. After one hit one of the big Aussie forwards said "Now twinkle little star".

It was inevitable that his home city of Leeds would eventually get hold of him and, although his nine seasons at Headingley may not have brought many trophies, few will deny that his contribution was immense. He is still understandably proud of his OBE awarded in 1994 and Man Of Steel achievement in 1991.

Leeds fans who had waited long to see his talent unfold got an instant payback with two tries on his debut against Auckland. He had the knack of turning games around almost single-handedly. He scored four tries against Wigan in 1988 and in the modern game there was surely no one better at the interception try. Time and time again his reading of the game, and the situation, made him one of the most exciting players of his generation.

In 1994 he was part of the Leeds team that played in its first Challenge Cup final for sixteen years. Ellery Hanley was the captain, and it was well known that the two did not get on well with each other.

Garry played 250 times for Leeds and scored 147 tries in that time. To watch his rapport with the fans was truly moving.

"It was so special", said Garry, "and I have never come close to anything like it either before Leeds or after the club. I will never forget coming back to face Leeds when I was coach of Huddersfield. I was given a standing ovation and I swear I was crying my eyes out."

I went on the Lions tour to Australia as rugby league correspondent for the newly formed Radio 5 in 1992. The whole tour was hit by controversy when Ellery Hanley, the captain, had to go home because of injury. Garry's role suddenly became even more important. His training and dedication to the cause was fantastic. He captained the side at Melbourne for the second Test and his inspirational performance led to a truly magnificent victory against all the odds. The whole match was broadcast live back home and apparently cheered up the all-night queuers at Wimbledon ahead of the tennis championships.

I spoke to Garry after the game and that familiar smile was wider than I had ever known.

"The greatest moment of my playing career", he told me. "We really outplayed them. The most complete team performance I have ever been involved with."

25
David Topliss

Andy Gregory, the great Wigan scrum-half, summed it up perfectly. "That was one of the nicest funerals I have ever been to. What a pity it was thirty years too soon."

We all felt like that on the day the rugby league family said its farewell to David Topliss. He was my age — just fifty-eight — when we lost him.

We thought he was indestructible. As a player he seemed that way. For Wakefield Trinity he gave his all. This is where the hallmark of a truly great sportsman is made. When I was at Radio Leeds, one of my regular Thursday night jobs was to do the rugby league round. I'd start at Leeds, move on to Castleford, then Featherstone and Wakefield. In all the years I was involved in the game 'Toppo' never refused an interview, no matter what had happened.

David Topliss.

That's why hundreds lined the streets for his Wakefield farewell. The cortège weaved its way through the crowds just like David did as a player.

Neil Fox, one of the gods of the game, remembered him with affection as the tears came to his eyes: "He would do anything for anybody. He was such a smashing bloke and a damned good player."

Garry Schofield played against him and with him so many times: "He was my mentor when I started out. I could always ask him for advice, and I admired and respected him enormously."

Although he didn't play in the final he was a member of England's World Cup winning squad in 1972. We have been so far behind the Aussies since then that this triumph takes on added

A youthful David Topliss.

meaning and significance. Throughout his career he scored 270 tries and is still the fifth highest scoring half-back behind Shaun Edwards, Alan Hardisty, Alex Murphy and Roger Millward.

He went on Ashes tours in 1973 and 1979, and captained great Britain against the Kangaroos in 1982. Later he coached the Great Britain under-21s in 1989.

For me the greatest memory of David was the Challenge Cup final replay at Elland Road in 1982. He scored two tries and, as captain, lifted the trophy. The team manager Arthur Bunting declared he "was my best ever buy".

*David Topliss (left) of Wakefield Trinity and Reg Bowden
of Widnes wrestle for the 1979 Challenge Cup; Trinity lost
the final 12-3.*

Inevitably people will reflect on his careers with Trinity
and Hull FC but his contribution elsewhere needs to be
noted. Oldham for example. Those who support the club
point to an incredible night back in 1986 when the so-
called 'Untouchables', the Kangaroos, were nearly beaten
and Toppo had a monumental game. Oldham actually
reached the semi-final of the Challenge Cup final that
year when they beat Wigan in the quarters but Topliss
missed the semi against Castleford because of a car acci-
dent and injury.

As a coach he had only fleeting success. I seem to
remember he won with Trinity the last ever Yorkshire Cup
competition in 1992-3. But his love for the game never
diminished. Andy Wilson the *Guardian*'s excellent rugby

David Topliss enjoyed an indian summer at Hull FC, signing for them in 1981 aged thirty-one for £15,000, and captained them to six finals in four years.

league writer made a telling point shortly after David's tragic death. "I can't remember watching a Wakefield match without Toppo being there. They should leave an empty seat for him to use when he wants to."

And he will. At every match.

26
Eddie Gray

I have always felt that Eddie Gray could so easily have become one of the greatest players in the world had he not been dogged by injury. His twenty-year association with Leeds United came to an end in 1985 after over 500 appearances, although he returned again ten years later.

I saw Eddie play on his debut on New Year's Day in 1966 and it heralded a career which led him to League Cup, Fairs Cup and Championship honours.

He is best remembered for the way he 'skinned alive' Chelsea's David Webb in the 1970 FA Cup Final. He sauntered past Webb countless times on that day only to see Leeds throw the tie away when goalkeeper Gary Sprake made one of his countless mistakes at crucial moments. The game ended 2-2, and Leeds lost the replay 2-1 at Old Trafford. One of the most exasperating aspects of Leeds under Revie was his total blind spot concerning Sprake.

"It was odd, I admit", says Eddie. "But people forget that Sprake also was a great keeper. That FA Cup Final boob was so depressing. We should have won the game by a mile. But let's not forget the save he made against Ferencvaros in the Fairs Cup Final a year or so before. One of the best I have ever seen and it led to us winning the cup."

David Webb of Chelsea is forced to back off yet again as Eddie Gray runs at him with the ball during the 1970 FA Cup Final.

Eddie Gray in action for Leeds United in the 1980-1 season. Eddie played over 500 times for Leeds over a twenty-year period.

Eddie's other memorable moment is still regarded as the greatest goal ever scored by a Leeds United player. It was against Burnley and, unlike other great goals, which are usually hallmarked by searing runs at pace in and

146

around defenders, this was crafted in no space at all. It started on the goal line where somehow he mesmerised two defenders, it continued in the penalty area where he feinted past other flailing defenders, before scoring with a measured shot. The match highlights were shown on Yorkshire Television, and the commentator Keith Macklin was unaware of how great a goal this was until he saw the replay.

Eddie has been a good friend of mine for many years. He is a thoroughly decent man and plays a very competitive round of golf, as I have found to my cost a few times.

His most challenging time came on his return to Leeds United in 1995. Previously he had managed the side after the club's relegation in 1982 under former Leeds star Allan Clarke. He was charged with getting the club promotion back into the top flight immediately, a challenge we all know which can never be taken for granted.

When he left Leeds in 1985 he had spells with Whitby Town, Rochdale and Hull City, before he was persuaded back in 1995 to look after United's up-and-coming youth talent. It was a good crop which Eddie nurtured well. Alan Smith, Ian Harte and Jonathan Woodgate all came through in what was a golden period for a while for the club.

But gold turned to rusty iron as the extravagances of the Leeds United board began to take their effect. Eddie's relationship with David O'Leary disintegrated and the upshot of many managerial changes led to Eddie being given 'mission impossible' in 2004 to save the club from relegation in the last few matches of the campaign.

It was a time of intense public scrutiny. Leeds fans could not accept that this team which had been playing Champions League football a year before was now sliding inexorably towards relegation.

But Eddie took all that scrutiny and criticism with dignity. The fans backed him all the way, knowing that he gave everything. I remember Sir Alex Ferguson in a press conference saying that he genuinely hoped Eddie could turn things round for the club. Praise indeed from a man not known for public utterances in this vein.

Recently, Eddie and I were discussing those forty-five days of Brian Clough which are now immortalised in the film *The Damned United*.

Clough took over from Revie in controversial circumstances and it is said that at his first meeting with the players he turned to Eddie and said "If you had been a racehorse, lad, I'd have had you shot."

Eddie confirmed this.

"Yes he did say that to me and to be honest it didn't worry me at all. But it really angered some of the other players who knew that I was very down about missing so many matches in my career, especially at this time."

His perception of Clough is fascinating:

"The Revie era came to an end so quickly, I think it left all of us stunned. We all knew Clough was a top-class manager but also that he didn't like our style of play. I honestly believe he thought he could shock us and make us his allies quickly. But this Leeds team was so full of dogged and, yes, difficult characters that it was a hopeless situation for him."

I have often talked to Eddie about his view on great sides and players. Leeds was and always will be his great love.

"We were a superb footballing side. We passed the ball around as good as any team and what people forget is that we didn't have any foreign players in the team, apart from us Scots.

"But I would love to have played in that fabulous Arsenal side known as the 'Invincibles', or dare I say Sir Alex Ferguson's team in recent years. I love both of those teams' philosophy of football: entertainment and attack."

He readily admits to an appreciation of Ronaldo:

"He is easily the best player in the world and he can score a goal at any stage of any game. Fabregas has a real instinctive touch about him too. He reminds me of Billy Bremner and Johnny Giles, with the way he can see an opening on the pitch where others can't."

Eddie was always approachable as a player and a manager. In my early years working for Radio Leeds you could guarantee he would do a few minutes for my programme. Indeed I can honestly say he never turned down any request from me.

These days he has become a top-class summariser. He still works for the club and their own digital radio station, and hosts a number of corporate days for the chairman Ken Bates.

It is sad to see Leeds languishing in the third tier of English football, but their fans are still right behind them. A staggering 37,000 turned up to watch their semi-final League One play-off against Millwall at the end of the 2008-9 season — evidence that the sleeping giant, once awakened, will be a force again in English football.

I hope Eddie will still be a part of that. He deserves to be.

27
Peter Elliott

Peter could justifiably have claimed to be in the wrong sport at the wrong time.

Why? Well how would you like to find your place in the midst of Steve Ovett and Steve Cram, not to mention Sebastian Coe? Not only did he establish himself, he also won a silver medal in the Seoul Olympics in the 1,500 metres.

Elliott was an old-fashioned athlete for most of his career. He worked as a joiner at British Steel, often starting his shift before 8am, and would train two or three times a day in an attempt to establish himself. He was always a brilliant talent. In 1977 he won the Northern Boys Cross-Country Championship and thus embarked on a wonderful career.

He had a distinctive running style which won him many friends, but not at one stage Sebastian Coe. More on that to come.

His running hit the top flight between 1983 and 1992, and in New Zealand he ran his first competitive 1,500 metres in an impressive time of 3:38:13. That set him up for Los Angeles and the 1984 Olympic Games. Both Steve Ovett and Steve Cram had been pre-selected for the games but the third spot was between Elliott or the

Olympic champion Seb Coe. Much was made of this showdown, with the winner told he would represent Great Britain in America.

In the *Look North* archives there is an interview with Peter before this race.

"I can't wait for it", he said. "It seems the fairest way of sorting out the problem of how to choose. It is a case of the best man on the day will go to LA."

The national papers were behind Seb Coe. Understandably I suppose, as he was the Olympic champion and Peter a young joiner from Rawmarsh.

It is important to set the scene for this decisive race. Coe was supremely confident and had not lost a race to anyone from Great Britain for eight years. He expected to win this one as well. But he didn't. Elliott stunned the country. Coe led for much of the race but Elliott took him at the end in a time of 3:39:66. Not a great time but one which Elliott thought had won him the 1,500 berth.

It didn't. The newspapers helped convince the selectors that Coe should still take the place and they were ultimately vindicated as Coe won the gold in LA. Elliott had to settle for an 800 metres place but injury put paid to any medal hopes.

Indeed Elliott missed the whole of 1985 through injury and at one stage was seriously worried that his career would abruptly end. He decided to concentrate on athletics full-time and the move paid off in the next few years. By the end of 1987 he'd notched up a silver in the World Championships and by the time the Seoul Olympics came he was in great shape for the 1,500 metres final.

I covered those Olympics, my first for the BBC, and made a plea to the editor to let me go to watch Peter's race in the fabulous stadium. Here I was really lucky. My

*Peter Elliott on track for a silver medal for Great Britain in the
1,500 metres at the 1988 Olympics in Seoul.*

pass took me trackside and as I had done a few features with Peter he recognised me in his warm-up and we had a brief chat.

"I'll do this for Yorkshire today, Harry", Peter said. "I'll go like the wind!"

What a race it was. A crowd of 80,000 packed in to see what is always one of the featured races. Remember Coe had retired now but the burden of responsibility was there. Peter came second to Kenya's Peter Rono, and he ran pretty quickly as well with a time of 3:36:15.

Peter received the MBE in 1990 and retired from running in 1992, but his involvement in sport is still as fresh as when he was pounding the track — he is now Regional Director (North) with the Institute of Sport in Sheffield.

28
Herol 'Bomber' Graham

He is generally ackowledged as one of the greatest fighters of all time never to win a world title. And I am sure that if Herol looks back on his career he would admit that it was largely his own fault. He went undefeated for thirty-eight fights, and held the British, Commonwealth and European middleweight titles. He lost his unbeaten record in a fight I witnessed against Sambu Kalambay who went on to become the world champion.

I followed his career with genuine enthusiasm. I liked him and in particular his trainer Brendan Ingle. Brendan of course is a legend in Sheffield. His gym has saved many kids from all kinds of disasters in life and I know he felt that Herol was a certain champion of the world.

Herol fought for the world title at middleweight and super-middleweight three times. He gave Mike McCallum, one of the greatest champions, one of his hardest fights in 1989 and only lost that on a split decision, mainly thanks to points deducted for low blows.

You could always recognise Herol in the ring. He fought with his hands low, and relied on his incredible speed and reflexes.

I once saw him do a charity turn where he invited members of the audience to try and knock his head off. It was

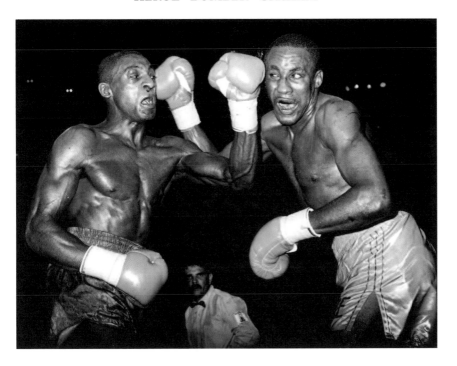

Herol 'Bomber' Graham and Mike McCallum feel each other's punching power during their WBA World Middleweight Championship fight at the Royal Albert Hall in May 1989. Herol gave McCallum one of the hardest fights of his career, but eventually lost on a split points decision.

hilarious, watching some fairly athletic opponents hitting fresh air as Herol moved away.

The best compliment given to Herol actually came from McCallum:

"He was a nightmare to fight. I knew I would lose unless I could slow him down. I eventually clocked him on the chin and that stopped him in his tracks. After that I took control."

There is little doubt that when Herol was in his prime those at the top avoided him. The list is as good as it gets:

Marvin Hagler, Sugar Ray Leonard and Roberto Duran all had chances to say they'd meet him; so too did the domestic boxing gods like Chris Eubank and Nigel Benn.

You can still witness Graham's worst moment on many boxing DVDs and TV compilation shows: his fight with Julian Jackson. It was going so well for Herol that he nearly stopped one of the most feared punchers in the game. Jackson had knocked out forty-nine of his opponents in his fifty-five wins but Herol seemed to be in line for a sensational win. Then he got caught by one of the most devastating punches ever thrown in any ring. He was out cold before he hit the canvas.

"I got over-confident", said Herol, "and when he hit me it took me nearly ten minutes to come round."

Despite this terrifying knock-out, which had him in hospital for some time after the event, Herol fought on.

He even got another shot at the world title in 1998 and again he was ahead. His opponent was the American Charles Brewer and at stake was the IBF super middleweight title. Herol was stopped in the tenth round.

His record at the end was broken with six defeats in all. But he knocked out twenty-eight of his fifty-four opponents. He was a great guy to interview, always bubbly. And he deserved a world title.

29
Adrian Moorhouse

My first Olympic Games was back in 1988 at Seoul in South Korea. I will never forget it for two reasons. My son Freddie was born while I was out there, and I was lucky to cover the gold medal win of Adrian Moorhouse.

I already knew Adrian well and had done features with him and his family for *Look North*. I am not sure anyone expected him to win gold, but they knew that this lad had Yorkshire grit and it was about time the county had another big success in the Olympics. Anita Lonsbrough (another Yorkshire Sporting Hero) was the last in 1960.

It is strange, isn't it, how we are all inspired by certain people who help us achieve our goals. Mine was David Coleman, the presenter of *Grandstand*. I thought he was the best in the business and I always wanted to be like him. Adrian wanted to emulate David Wilkie who, of course, won gold in the breaststroke in Montreal in 1976.

In a preview piece I did with Adrian before Seoul he told me about his Wilkie admiration:

"David was holding a swimming clinic in Liverpool. I was thirteen and my parents gave me the £50 to go for swimming lessons with him. He asked at the end of the session who wanted to win a gold medal at the Olympics. I put my hand up, cocky so-and-so that I was."

Adrian clearly got much help from his coach at Leeds swimming club, Terry Dennison. He never had any doubt about Adrian.

"He was such a determined young lad", said Terry. "Really conscientious about training and as I was a very demanding coach he probably thought I gave him little back. In truth I didn't."

Adrian reflects that as a young lad he was 'Billy-no-mates': "I was so determined that most of my friends gave up on me."

In truth he nearly gave up on himself as well when he finished fourth in Barcelona in the Olympic Games. "It took me a good few months to get over that, but then I was so focused."

Prior to Seoul, Adrian had established himself as the number one in the 100 metres for three years. His main rival was a Russian called Dmitri Volkov. When the final came, Moorhouse found himself sixth at the turn and Volkov was under world record pace. But within a few metres of the second lap he was catching him.

"He seemed to be moving backwards. He was knackered. But I was totally unaware of the Hungarian Karoly Guttler. He was on me stroke for stroke."

In the end, Adrian won gold by 0.01 of a second.

His triumph in Seoul was one of the most heartwarming moments I have enjoyed in my career. I was with his mum and dad, and watched them go through all kinds of torment during the final. If you could have seen their joy at the end of it all — it was so special.

We take for granted the commitment athletes make, but we forget about the mums and dads. The financial side of it is one thing. But running your kid to and from the pool at unearthly hours day in day out is another.

Adrian Moorhouse raises his arms in celebration at winning the 100 metres breaststroke gold medal at the 1988 Olympics. I was lucky enough to watch the final in Seoul with Adrian's mum and dad, and their happiness was just as ecstatic.

What I like about Adrian is that although he is still heavily involved in the sport as a first-class swimming commentator, it is only a very small part of his life. He is a successful businessman these days and, as ever, a thoroughly decent chap.

30
Anita Lonsbrough

Up until the 2008 Olympics and Rebecca Adlington's success, Anita Lonsbrough was the most famous English swimmer of all time. She was from Huddersfield and her story is one of the most memorable.

I interviewed her twenty years ago about the level of commitment she put into her success. She told of training sessions before school at 5am in the morning. Every day. She would often open up the pool herself and trudge relentlessly, lap after lap, usually in really cold water. She talked passionately about her experiences at Cambridge Road pool when she would appeal to the boilerman there to get rid of the cockroaches before she would dive in.

In 1962 Anita became the first woman to win the BBC Sports Personality of the Year award. This was two years after she had won gold in Rome. The last three in the running for the award were all women: Dorothy Hyman, the athlete from South Yorkshire; another swimmer, Linda Ludgrove; and Anita. They were all told to prepare a speech if they won.

"I never thought of winning", she said. "They announced it in the usual way. 'In third place, Dorothy Hyman; in second, Linda Ludgrove...', and then it all went in slow motion. I couldn't grasp what I had achieved."

*Anita Lonsbrough in training at Cambridge Road Baths,
Huddersfield, in 1963.*

Anita had won two gold medals in the Commonwealth Games in Sydney in 1958 and was also the world record holder, but she'd been overtaken in the build-up to the 1960 Rome Olympics by Wiltrud Urselmann from Germany. No one really expected Anita to even make it to Rome. She had battled with gastro-enteritis, flu and even a vicious insect bite. But she recounts a trip to the Trevi fountain:

"The song rang out at me: *Three Coins in a Fountain*. So I tossed them in and wished ... I got a gold return from those pennies."

Anita at home with her 1962 BBC Sports Personality of the Year award.

The race itself was thrilling. Anita edged past Urselmann and then in the last few metres the German came back but Lonsbrough hung on by a whisker.

"It makes me laugh when I look back on the race", she recalled, "to hear the BBC commentator screaming at me because at the time I had no idea how close a call it was.

"When I was on the podium, I wondered if I was in some kind of dream and that I would wake up. It was a really odd feeling."

Mind you, after that she did know what had hit her: interview after interview, a champagne reception from the British Olympic Committee and, a really lovely touch, a red carpet made of towels laid out by her team-mates.

Anita passes on her swimming knowledge to another generation of Yorkshire children.

"They caught all my tears. I don't think anyone can really appreciate what it is like to hear the national anthem playing and know that it is because of you."

When she returned to Huddersfield she received a heroine's welcome. But in the true tradition of what amateur meant in those days, she was soon back at her work in a local government office.

A heroine's welcome from the people of Huddersfield at the civic reception to celebrate Anita's 1960 Olympic victory.

She was awarded the MBE for services to swimming in 1963 and the following year was the first female Olympic flag-bearer during the opening ceremony at the Tokyo Olympics.

Olympic success these days brings riches. Not so then for Anita, but it did open doors. One in particular. What no one knew at the time was that on the way to Tokyo in 1964 she had met the 4,000-metre cycling champion Hugh Porter. Hugh then had another chase on his hands to catch Anita. In 1965 they were married and, as a token of the town's appreciation for all she had done for Huddersfield, she was given the town hall for free for her wedding reception.

When she retired, her life took another turn: "I became a journalist and commentated for the BBC for many years. All the hard work did one great thing for me: it gave me a good life."

My favourite Yorkshire sports grounds

My father told me that he was there when Odsal Stadium claimed the world record crowd for a rugby league match at the Warrington v Halifax Challenge Cup Final replay on the 5th May 1954. The official attendance was 102,569 but unofficial estimates range from 120,000 to over 150,000.

What is certain is that these days the grounds are immeasurably more luxurious and safe. But I was brought up at a time when luxury was far from the reality.

In my career with the BBC I have been lucky enough to visit the best stadia in the world. My first Olympics in 1988 took me to Seoul in South Korea where countless buildings sprang up to host a truly outstanding games.

For me the best of them all was the Australian experience in 2000. Sitting in the Olympic Stadium in Sydney, I suddenly realised how far we had come in the space of some twenty years. The tragedies at Hillsborough and Valley Parade changed the face of new sports stadia.

Yet for me I still have so much affection for the grounds I was brought up in. I could have easily named ten in this section alone, rather than just five.

I have always loved Hillsborough, still one of the greatest in the country and synonymous with the World Cup in

1966 and wonderful FA Cup semi-finals. Elland Road and the 'Scratching Shed' is hardly likely to win prizes for aesthetic beauty but waiting for the turnstiles to open at 1.30pm before the three o'clock kick off and being squashed for the next four and a half hours is still a lasting impression, in more ways than one.

I can list even more sports grounds that have special associations for me: Thrum Hall, the home of Halifax rugby league; Fartown, once the home of Huddersfield rugby league and county cricket; and Acklam Park, Middlesbrough, where I first cut my teeth commentating on Yorkshire cricket.

I have narrowed my selection, though, to the grounds which built up my Yorkshire pride in all sports. Three, sadly, are no more, but the echoes of great achievements are there for all to remember, and will ensure, I hope, that they will never be forgotten.

Park Avenue, Bradford

When you look at the history of Yorkshire County Cricket Club it is fair to say that it has moved around a bit. I have been trying to find out just how many grounds have hosted Yorkshire matches. In alphabetical order, I think this is a fairly accurate list: Abbeydale (Sheffield), Barnsley, Bradford (Park Avenue), Bramall Lane (Sheffield), Darnall, Dewsbury, Great Horton Road (Bradford), Hall Park (Horsforth), Harrogate, Headingley, Holbeck, Huddersfield, Hull, Hunslet, Middlesbrough (three different grounds, the most notable being Acklam Park), Saville Park (Castleford), Scarborough, Thrum Hall (Halifax), Wakefield and York.

One or two of these have special associations for me, none more so than Bradford Park Avenue.

I have so many happy childhood memories of watching football at Bradford Park Avenue. Here, Park Avenue's Bill Elliott (in white) jumps for a header against Arsenal during the FA Cup third round tie in January 1948.

We are understandably proud of our history here in Yorkshire. But there are a number of sad chapters which don't reflect well on that heritage. None more so than what happened at Park Avenue, not once but twice.

My father and elder brother brought me up as a Park Avenue supporter. I loved going to the ground to watch soccer. The old stand, if memories serve me right, gave a great view.

The club always seemed to live in the shadow of Bradford City. And like all great derby rivalries, there were sets of supporters on both sides of the city who refused to even visit their opponents' ground.

The first game I ever went to was in the mid-1950s when Blackpool were the visitors. My dad had built up my expectations but I can still feel to this day the sense of nervousness I experienced when the team trotted out.

In 1961 the club installed floodlights and the occasion was marked by a game against Czechoslovakia. Seven of the Czech players went on to play for their country in the following year's World Cup in Chile.

Jimmy Scoular had a big impact on the Park Avenue club in his role as player-manager. My dad often said he was the hardest player he had ever seen. That balding head was difficult to ignore from my vantage point in the stand.

But my main recollections surround the great Kevin Hector. I was his number one fan when his goalscoring prowess began. The Saturday ritual with my brother was tried and tested. We'd moved to Leeds in 1960 so the train to Forster Square was followed by the walk to Park Avenue. I always sat in the stand in my dad's seat as he worked on Saturdays.

Hector was a revelation. He scored 100 league goals by the time he was twenty-one. Only Jimmy Greaves and Dixie Dean achieved the same feat faster. He was sold to Derby County in 1966-7 for £34,000 and the money should have been used to stabilise the club, but it wasn't.

When the chairman and benefactor Herbert Metcalfe died a few years later the club's future ended too. This great ground was sold in 1973.

Years later in a special programme for *Look North* we went back. How sad to see the stand gone and the terraces covered in weeds. A lost opportunity. For me dual grounds have so much character.

The record crowd at Park Avenue, by the way, was a

staggering 34,000 for a game against Blackpool. (Back in 1931 a game agains Leeds United on Christmas Day recorded a crowd of over 34,000. This was amended to 32,429 when it was found that quite a few had been counted twice.)

I am indebted to my close friend John Helm for one or two other interesting snippets about the Park Avenue ground. Syd Dickinson scored twice direct from a corner in a game against Burnley in 1931. In 1941 during the Second World War, two matches were played by Park Avenue on the same day, Christmas Day. The first was against York City, which they drew in the morning, and the second to Huddersfield, which they lost in the afternoon, 3-1.

RIP, Bradford Park Avenue ... all that remains of the ground today.

Even earlier than this though, in 1927, the club won its twenty-fifth consecutive home match in Division Three (North) and this is still a record for any club in the Football League.

If we go back to 1909 there are more little gems to unearth. England played Ireland in an international match. The programme cost 1d and there were lucrative adverts for Marfleet's cold and cough cure, Tidswell's artificial teeth and Corsican cigarettes. Wonderful. England won the match 4-0, with 25,000 people there.

When the cricket was lost as well it was a double blow. The Victorian pavilion was surely one of the finest sights

For me, Bradford Park Avenue was the most 'Yorkshire' of all the county cricket club's grounds, particularly with its splendid Victorian pavilion.

in cricket. There are still many of us who feel that the Park Avenue ground was the most 'Yorkshire' of all county's cricket venues. From 1880 to 1996, when the curtain was finally closed on the cricket history of the ground, 314 matches at first-class level had been played. It is well known that Sir Len Hutton and Herbert Sutcliffe loved playing there.

Park Avenue fell foul of Yorkshire because no one would take responsibility for its upkeep. It became victim to vandalism and the terracing was unsafe. What a sad end. I can remember reading a great piece by Bill Bridge of the *Yorkshire Post* on its demise a few years ago. Bill based his article around Bob Appleyard who used to race from school in the 1930s to watch his heroes play, and all for ten shillings and sixpence for the whole season. That would include at least three championship matches.

The first ever championship match was in 1881 when Kent were the visitors. A year before that the Players of the North faced the touring Australians.

David 'Bluey' Bairstow loved the place. He once made 122 on what was the last championship match played there in 1985. I'm reminded, too, of one incident when Middlesex were playing. The match was very tight, and Clive Radley bravely came in with nine men down despite a broken arm. His side needed two to win and Bluey stumped him.

There was a reprieve a few years later thanks to the enthusiasm of Appleyard and local pharmacist Geoff Moss, and four more seasons were wrung out of the dregs.

Yorkshire, though, were into a fairly harsh cull of grounds by then. They wanted Headingley (understandably) to be the home ground but were prepared to allow Scarborough its share of games because it gave the county the best attendances of the whole season. The Harrogate cricket festival was also a victim and by 1996 any hope of returning cricket to Bradford was finally over.

Bramall Lane

There are two great stories I have heard regularly about cricket at Bramall Lane. One concerns Dickie Bird, the other Fred Trueman. One of them is probably true.

Yorkshire were playing the West Indies there in the 1960s. The tourists had as their opening attack Wes Hall and Charlie Griffith. Fred came in to bat to face Wes who was on his full run-up. As Wes approached, Fred stopped him in his tracks and asked for the sightscreen to be moved.

"Where would you like it?"

"Between me and that mad so-and-so running in", was Fred's reply.

Dickie's version is surprisingly similar.

Let's be honest about Bramall Lane: it was by no means an attractive setting. At its pomp the sightscreen in the middle of the football pitch was hardly welcoming. But it was still a great ground and when it stopped hosting championship games in 1973 a rich tapestry of Yorkshire history was lost. In the early days of the county cricket club it was virtually its home, until the club moved to Leeds in 1903.

From my many visits there, especially in the 1960s when my love of cricket really started, the knowledge of the Bramall Lane crowd was legendary.

The trouble with it as a venue, of course, was obvious. It is impossible to have a football pitch and a top-quality cricket pitch side by side. Originally the site was chosen for its bright aspect and clean air. How ironic that was because by 1900, with industries blasting out more toxic air than has ever been known, it was a ground which always had a special atmosphere and we are not talking one of anticipation or excitement.

But it did host what was called a Victory Test match in 1945 against the Aussies. Poor attendances put paid to this ever being repeated, especially when England lost by 143 runs and the bad light experienced throughout the whole match was blamed. The Victory Test featured Keith Miller for Australia, and for England the great Wally Hammond.

The Aussies actually played there again on tour in 1948. Bradman played and when word got out that he was about to bat it is said that many hundreds in the steel-works left work just to get a glimpse of him at the crease.

No one really watches championship cricket these days. But back in the 1940s, after the Second World War, the attendances were nothing short of remarkable: 22,000, for example, turned up in 1947 to watch the Roses match.

Conditions then were, to say the least, primitive. Most of those who can cast their minds back over sixty years will recall that they sat on concrete football terracing or splinter-ridden wooden benches. Today, Health and Safety would have closed the ground in an instant.

In 1968 Yorkshire beat the Aussies at the Lane by an innings, and apparently after the match the spectators were treated to a ball-throwing contest involving quite a few of the players from both teams. Incidentally, do you know who captained Yorkshire on this memorable occasion? One Fred Trueman. Fred told me that not one committee man said anything to him for his astute captaincy on that day, which still goes down as one of the greatest in Yorkshire history.

But those recent memories are nothing when you delve deeper into people's memories.

It is said that Douglas Jardine received a standing ovation all the way to the wicket in 1933 as the crowd's way of showing appreciation for the way the controversial Bodyline tour had gone for England the year before. Jardine made a century in the second innings there and his quote still lives on:

"I wish I had been a Yorkshireman if this is what their supporters are like."

Yorkshire's final game at the ground was in 1973, and in the same year the football club built a new stand and another chapter of Yorkshire's sporting heritage ended. The last match was a Roses clash. The last ball ever faced there fell to Colin Johnson.

I can recall chairing a cricket society meeting in Sheffield when we had a night of nostalgia. It was held at Abbeydale which became an occasional home for the county cricket club in South Yorkshire to appease the legions of members who were upset at the loss of the Lane. One man recollected that final year, 1973. His season pass for the ground was £1 5s and for that he got "four 'decent' matches" — a Roses match, Surrey or Middlesex and usually Leicestershire or Northants. Thrown in was a coaching session from George Pope.

The steelworks provided the mainstay of the Lane support and, because it was a twenty-four-hour-a-day industry, shift workers would call in at some stage on their way to the steelworks.

"It was great", the man recalled. "The workers would often leave their bottles behind and we'd get threepence for returning them. As for the cushions, they were worth 2s 6d."

Sheffield children take a piece of cricketing history after Yorkshire's last match at Bramall Lane in 1973.

There were so many stories rattled off in this meeting. One man asked Close for an autograph on an old picture of him. "Fancy getting me to sign this. Clear off. " He had been bowled out for a duck.

Another memory was then ignited. Apparently there was a real character who sold scorecards. Arthur Smith was his name. I know because in the archives of *Look North* one of my predecessors did a feature on him. He was always visible because he wore a white smock and his newspaper-seller's delivery was unmistakable:

"Scorecards. Get your scorecards here. I have the team news ahead of the *Star* and it's accurate too."

That's why he was known to stalwarts as the 'Voice'.

He was well known all over the county scene by Yorkshire's fans and unless I am mistaken he used to take his wife to all the matches as well.

You just don't get characters like Arthur around these days, do you? For me Arthur goes hand in hand with grounds like Bramall Lane.

North Marine Road, Scarborough

In July 2005 I was invited for lunch to the Scarborough Cricket Festival by Cec Snell, the chief executive, and Bill Mustoe, chairman of the Scarborough club. They live, breathe and eat cricket at Scarborough. At the end of the lunch, they asked me if I would fancy being president of the festival in the following year. I was stunned and, in truth, deeply moved.

For me to follow in the footsteps of people like Sir Michael Parkinson, Dickie Bird, Sir Tim Rice and Sir Lawrence Byford, and that's just a short selection of greats, was an honour I couldn't refuse.

The festival, referred to by me as the World's Greatest, must be preserved at all costs. Its heyday was the Edwardian era when matches were easy to organise and money not so important. Not so today. Finance is clearly a problem. Yorkshire's understandable desire to play at Headingley, which they own, cannot be disputed. But neither can the role of Scarborough.

It is a ground that has changed little in the last fifty years. The pavilion is still an imposing structure and, while the terracing needs upgrading, I defy anyone to get a better view of cricket anywhere in the country.

In the old days, all touring teams would end the summer at Scarborough. I heard recently an interview by Charles Place of the *Scarborough Evening News* with a

The Scarborough Cricket Festival has been one of Yorkshire's great sporting occasions for over a century.

former president, Don Robinson. Don did an immense amount for the festival at a time when it was under threat. His early experiences, though, are something most of us can only dream about.

Back in 1946, Don got what must have been a dream job for an eleven year old: cleaning the dressing rooms. Playing that year at the festival was Sir Donald Bradman. The other Don (Robinson) got his autograph and carried the great man's bag to what was then one of the finest hotels in Europe, the Grand.

"I was so excited to carry his bags", recalled Don. "But when I got to the hotel they wouldn't let me in. Such was the grandeur of the place."

That moment had a big influence on Don's role as president. He was determined to make an impact and was responsible for enticing the great Dennis Lillee to play at the festival during his first year of office.

When I took over for two years in 2006 Don told me also to make an impact. Well I am not sure I did, but we did make a DVD of the history of the event which sold well.

We uncovered some remarkable facts in the research for the DVD. I met a group of surgeons and doctors who come to the festival every year and offer their services, should they be needed, for nothing.

I also met George who hadn't missed a festival for sixty years. "I love walking to the ground from my hotel and mingling with the crowds", George told me. "The chatter is always about cricket or the weather. 'Should we bat if we win the toss?' and so on."

The wonderful J M Kilburn, who wrote with distinction for years for the *Yorkshire Post*, penned a superb article on why the Scarborough Cricket Festival had a place in his heart:

"Is there a more beautiful phrase in the English language than 'cricket in Scarborough'? The slow walk to the match, preferably taking in the sea view and a lumpen bag choked with food. The first drink could be taken at noon..." In truth many people start drinking well before.

Dickie Bird never misses the festival. He stays in the same hotel and is without a doubt the best-known figure who troops around the stadium every day.

While I was enjoying my presidency, Dickie's foundation looked after the one part of the festival which I think needs attention: the Monday. The problem is quite simply money, but I did try to bring over some real stars for a one-day match during my second year in office. I really tried. But the fees some of these guys were asking of £1,000 plus expenses made it impossible to finance.

Howzat!... with Dickie Bird at the Scarborough Cricket Festival.

The cricket ground at North Marine Road, Scarborough, in the 1950s, with a packed crowd for the Cricket Festival.

The festival has such a fabulous history. The club secured its tenancy at North Marine Road back in 1863 and the festival itself began in 1876 attracting the great W G Grace and other top cricketers. It didn't get its first county match until 1896 when Leicestershire were the visitors, but the tradition of top-class games was established and never wavered after that. In 1926 it held a festival jubilee and a lavish banquet at the opulent Grand Hotel.

One of the great traditions of the festival concerns those players who have hit a six and cleared the boarding houses which surround the ground on Trafalgar Square. WG Grace is said to have done it and so too is the Australian Cec Pepper. That was in 1945. To my knowledge it has not been achieved since in a festival match.

There's a wonderful gesture always available for cricketers at Scarborough to have their name etched in history for all time: the honours board. Set up by Cec Snell and Bill Mustoe, any player who scores a century or takes five wickets in the first-class match gets his name in the dressing room. It's a great idea and one which distinguishes Scarbrough from so many grounds.

There have certainly been some memorable moments to record. In the old days, of course, the festival would have as part of the programme a visiting guest's eleven. Names such as H D G Leverson Gower may not exactly roll off the tongue but Tom Pearce, Brian Close and Sir Michael Parkinson most definitely do.

I have mentioned already the problem the festival has on one of its days because of the financial restraints, but in the 1970s, '80s and '90s it held a one-day competition involving four counties.

Prior to that in 1925 there was the greatly loved Gentlemen versus Players match. Sir Jack Hobbs scored 266 in this match held back in 1925. A viewer to *Look North* sent me an old cine reel which actually showed Hobbs playing at Scarborough and coaching young cricketers on the pitch. There were even a few frames of him relaxing at his host's home in the town.

What incredible days those were and they showed us why the superstars of cricket in those days were so in touch with their public.

Sir Len Hutton loved the whole seaside experience as well. In 1951, also in the Gentlemen versus Players match, he hit 241. Ken Rutherford, the former New Zealand Test match cricketer, scored 317 against Brian Close's eleven in 1986. The great Wilf Rhodes took 9-24 back in 1899 against the touring Aussies.

My own love affair with the ground and the festival was cemented by two events that I will never forget. In 1994 I left the BBC for a year to take a post as the Rugby League's public affairs executive. An unhappy experience.

But to cheer myself up I took my wife-to-be, Helen, to Scarborough for a day at the cricket. You see, I do know how to treat the ladies. What a match we chose. Surrey beat Yorkshire in a forty-over match by scoring an astonishing 375-4, Alistair Brown and Graham Thorpe both making centuries.

Our next trip there together (I went every year on a solo basis) was 2001 where we saw what, for me, was the greatest exhibition of batting I am ever likely to witness. Darren Lehmann made 191 but the statistics were almost mind-blowing: he hit twenty fours and eleven sixes; he only faced 103 balls; and was only at the crease for 115 minutes. From this moment on I have never had a problem taking Helen to cricket, especially to the home of the World's Greatest cricket festival.

The ground even passes the ultimate test from the members of the press. Is there a better location for an après box anywhere in county cricket? I suspect not.

Just to round off my own Scarborough experience, I also saw David Byas on his home ground score a double century in 1995 when Yorkshire made 600-4 against Worcestershire.

I love every inch of the place.

Headingley

There are two people in broadcasting and journalism that I revere: Des Lynam and Michael Parkinson. Parky's chat shows still set the standards and so too does his brilliant writing. But I do disagree with him on the subject of

Headingley. Michael openly admits that he has no love for the place and says it's the lack of an imposing pavilion that is one of the reasons for this.

However, along with Dickie Bird I share one common denominator with Sir Michael. We both went for trials at the club and suffered similar fates.

In his Yorkshire trial, Dickie Bird actually went for nets with Parky. Legend had it that you hoped to be invited into Maurice Leyland's net and not Arthur Mitchell's. Inevitably Dickie got into that of Mitchell who was scathing about all and sundry. Dickie tells the story that he was facing Bob Appleyard and Fred Trueman. (Remember all this was happening in front of the old winter sheds and the crowds of people who would turn up to view the pretenders.) Dickie said he was bowled out loads of times on a "vicious track". Arthur Mitchell meandered down the wicket and asked: "Hey lad, what's tha job?"

"I am a joiner down the pit," said Dickie.

"Well you'd better go back and build something that'll protect you from those bowlers, lad."

There are two reasons why I place Headingley at the very top of my sporting venues: cricket and rugby league. Twin sporting arenas these days are rare. Double international venues are priceless.

However, the relationship between the cricket and rugby league rulers of the ground have not been cordial. Yorkshire resented their role as tenants, although in truth they had plenty of opportunities in the past to do something about it long before Colin Graves took it on himself to sort out the mess once and for all.

A few short years ago Yorkshire County Cricket Club faced ruin. Its status as a Test match venue was being questioned almost yearly. The only way it could survive was for the county to own its own section of the ground and make it pay.

Unashamedly I have always championed the cause of Headingley as a Test match ground. I always will. It is the stadium where some of the most dramatic Test matches of all time have taken place, beginning in 1899 when the Australians played there.

I once spoke at length to Fred Trueman about the ground, which of course had a special appeal for him.

"I loved the place on Test match morning", Fred told me. "There were always hundreds of spectators queueing outside from about seven o'clock and we often would stop to talk to some of them as we went in."

Difficult to see that happening in this day and age, isn't it?

People usually associate the ground as a seam bowler's paradise and one which unusually would swing as cloud conditions became overcast. But the ground is also renowned for some great feats of batting.

It witnessed two utterly superb triple centuries by the incomparable Don Bradman of Australia, in 1930 and again on his return in 1934. Bradman was back in 1948. My brother recounted that he went with our dad and sat where the old winter shed used to be. At this time the Aussies were invincible. They had devoured everything that had come before them and the queues to get into the ground started at seven in the morning.

Geoffrey Boycott used the setting to achieve his 100th century in first-class cricket in 1977. The ovation from the 18,000 Yorkshire crowd lasted six minutes and thirty-two seconds. I was commentating on Radio Leeds at the time and we timed it. I can remember my sports editor saying down the line: "For God's sake say something, Harry". On reflection he was probably right.

For me the mark of a great sports stadium is one which is an international venue in two different sports: Headingley is one.

Four years later another incredible experience: the Ian Botham Test. England came back from the brink of defeat against Australia, thanks to Ian's fantastic century and the fastest spell of bowling Bob Willis has ever delivered as he took eight wickets to rattle out the Aussies in their second innings.

I have never really understood why there has been a media campaign against the ground. Much of this has actually come from former players who performed well there. Well, now they have little room for complaint. The new plans, which again are the inspiration of Colin Graves, will allow the media to create their own state-of-the-art press and TV centre. The new pavilion will, if all goes to plan, be the very best in the world.

All anyone needs to do is look at Headingley ten years ago and see what it is today to realise what has been achieved. Maybe Sir Michael will have another take on the ground when this is completed.

Although Test matches inevitably take all the headlines, one innings I saw will forever last in my memory. Sadly there should have been 20,000 watching but the crowd was around 2,000. The date: Thursday 21st September 2006. Yorkshire were playing Durham in a match they had to win to stay in the First Division of the county championship. I was privileged to be allowed access to the dressing room after an innings which brought tears to my eyes and that of the other 1,999 souls who witnessed it: Darren Lehmann made 339. Just two short of George Hirst's 101-year-old record. I will swear to this day that Darren gave his wicket away at that point. He was certainly aware of the record but such was his bond with the Yorkshire members that I am sure he felt that the record should stay for a Yorkshireman not an Aussie.

David Byas said to me after the great man had been dismissed to an emotional standing ovation:

"I have never seen a better batting display than this. This guy has everything and when he attacks a bowler he utterly destroys him. His range of shots is freakish."

After Darren had staggered into the dressing room totally and utterly exhausted, he lit a cigarette and out poured real emotion.

"I felt out there today something unique in sport", he told me. "The Headingley crowd willed me to bat like that. I felt like a tyke and to do it here, where Australia's hero Sir Don Bradman scored a triple century twice, fills me with pride. Eee bye gum, Harry, I feel like a Yorkie."

Darren loved playing at Headingley.

These days Headingley's Test match future is assured on the rota. But there are many of us who feel that it should always be there whatever the Test match, whatever the year. Colin Graves has done great service to the county and, if all of his plans are successful, Headingley has a rich future ahead of it.

Leeds Road, Huddersfield

I know that everyone raves these days about how great the new grounds are and how they cater for the spectator in a way the old relics didn't. But how many give us the atmosphere?

Don't get me wrong, I love the new Wembley and it is undeniably more luxurious than the old place. I also like to go to the Galpharm which is the new-ish home of Huddersfield Town and the Giants.

But for atmosphere it just can't compare with Leeds Road. I loved to go to the ground. I cut my teeth there in broadcasting terms and to this day I have never been better looked after at half time than I was there.

In my early days at Radio Leeds there was a ritual we performed every Thursday and Friday. Under John Helm's leadership we did the rounds. It was just accepted that the managers of Halifax Town, Huddersfield Town and Bradford City would let us interview them for our sports programmes.

I was very lucky with Huddersfield Town. Ian Greaves was certainly one of the most decent men I have ever met in sport. He would always welcome us into his office at Leeds Road with a cup of tea and a biscuit. So too would George Mulhall and Micky Buxton. I loved Micky. He used to ramble on about all sports, but one day he just stopped the recording and uttered these words: "Have you ever thought just how many great players have played here on this Leeds Road ground?"

I decided to do a half-hour radio special to see how many I could track down who were still living at the time and also record their memories of the stadium.

Denis Law was known as the king and I had the pleasure of spending a few weeks with him during the Mexico World Cup in 1986 where he was one of the summarisers. We talked about his early days at Leeds Road and how he established a special bond with the place.

"I joined Huddersfield in 1955 and I looked like a stick", Denis told me. "I also had a squint and players often mocked me because I couldn't see. So I had my eyes sorted and my life changed. I loved playing the second half attacking the Leeds Road end of the ground."

He only made eighty-one appearances for Town but under the legendary Bill Shankly became a player of true class. His debut was in 1956 against Notts County and he left in 1960 for a British record fee of £55,000 to go to Manchester City. I asked him what was special about Leeds Road:

"It was a classic football ground and you knew you were stepping out to something special when the roar of the crowd hit you. Bill Shankly also told me that, here in Yorkshire at Huddersfield, they will tell you straight what you are like. They did."

Digging out that programme from Radio Leeds, I stumbled across an interview I did with one of the true characters of Leeds Road, still revered today: Frank Worthington. This man was a remarkable talent, nurtured by Ian Greaves. Ian, though, knew what he was creating:

"He was so lazy. Exasperating, and yet I saw him do things at Leeds Road that no one could do."

Huddersfield Town fans celebrate Simon Baldry's early goal during the last match at Leeds Road on the 30th April 1994.

Frank's talent was recognised by the Huddersfield Town fans in the 1969-70 season. Frank played every match. Remarkable really when you consider he was the target, because of the flamboyant way he played, for crunching tackles. I once saw him score a goal against Blackpool where he beat four men with one drop of the shoulder, before scoring from thirty yards.

He loved too his time at Leeds Road and there are pictures of him plastered over the walls of the new stadium. "There are some of me sober too", he told me recently.

My favourite Yorkshire sporting traditions

I know of no county which can boast so many traditions which started here. I have often wondered how and why Yorkshire has been the birthground of so many. It must be the spirit of the county and, I believe, our competitive spirit. The battles in history between Yorkshire and the rest are well known. We have blown away the Scots, the Lancastrians and many others, and since then we have always had to justify ourselves. What better way than in unique challenges and defying all-comers to see if they can beat us.

"You can tell a Yorkshireman, but not much." How true.

So here are five sporting traditions which still hang on to their birthplace. I can hardly say they will get sponsorship which will take them into a 'super league', but for me they sum up what is best about this place. We love a battle of wits, brawn and skill.

Boxing Day cricket at North Leeds

A good few years ago I was asked to play in this match and I took it so seriously I even went for a net on Christmas Eve. I need not have bothered. I was out first ball, caught at mid-off in a run chase. That's my version.

The truth was it was so cold I never saw the ball at all and I was bowled middle stump. The match though is in need of a boost. It ain't what it used to be and with only 100 souls turning up in recent years, you can see why.

The inspiration for the game came from someone I knew well, Ron Yeomans. The first match was actually organised for Seacroft near Leeds in 1948, but it did not take place until the following year at Collingham between Wetherby and Leeds. At a dinner recently in Wetherby, I spoke to a man who actually went to this game. George Coles is in his nineties now and lives in Bradford.

"It was a wonderful occasion", said George. "I think that there was a crowd of 3,000. One of the sides was captained by the fomer England player Maurice Leyland. He made thirty very quickly and got a great ovation as he came out."

After this, Boxing Day cricket became a regular fixture in the calendar of the Northern Cricket Society. But it became nomadic, with Whitkirk, Bramhope, Alwoodley and Boston Spa hosting the extravaganza.

But my research inadvertently trawled up a remarkable game held in 1955 which my father saw. The setting was Alwoodley. At the time I was five, and my mum and dad were living in Bradford. My father loved his cricket and persuaded my long-suffering mother that a trip to a cricket match on Boxing Day would be a great idea. I was thrilled, not knowing what on earth would happen.

The game began at 11am on a cricket mat at the ground. It was a time match. Three hours was allocated. The Northern Cricket Society batted first and made 82-8. Why and how do I know this? My dad played. He was a wicketkeeper/batsman and scored twenty-two. I was so proud of him. Then Alwoodley went into bat and with

'Snow stopped play' is not a phrase you are likely to see in a cricket match report, except perhaps for the Boxing Day cricket match at North Leeds — and even then the match has gone ahead in several feet of snow.

the score 21-5, the snow fell in such volume that the game was abandoned. The next year it snowed even more.

There is one wonderful story concerning a super cricketer called Arthur Booth. This man topped the county and England bowling averages in 1946. He set off to play in the game from his home in Manchester by car. The car as he put it 'conked out', right on top of the Pennines. He thumbed a lift with his cricket bag very much in view. His benefactor was a Yorkshire farmer, who said to him:

"Where tha from, lad? Lancashire eh? Cricket season's well over. Mind you that lot can't laik anyway."

These are memories I treasure.

Today the tradition is maintained at North Leeds Cricket Club and they pride themselves on playing a match whatever the weather.

Over the years some superb cricketers have graced the event. Brian Close was a regular for many years, but other notaries include Yorkshire colleague Don Wilson and Nottinghamshire's Brian Bolus. One of my favourites, though, was Johnny Lawrence. When I was at Leeds Grammar School before I moved to St Peter's School in York, I used to go every Saturday morning for nets with Johnny at Rothwell. His record in the Boxing Day event must be one of the most impressive. Between 1949 and 1964 he played in every game.

Other notaries who've turned out in recent years include Geoff Cope, Chris Old, Tim Boon and Jim Love. For the record, North Leeds hosted their first match in 1973 and the game was won off the last ball, as indeed it was in the following year as well.

By far and away the most impressive event, though, was 1981. On this occasion the game was played in three feet of snow. How the Northern Cricket Society managed to make 108 in these conditions is still a mystery. But it tells you lots about Yorkshire grit and determination, if nothing else.

Quoits

I have covered a multitude of sports for *Look North* and *Grandstand* over the years, and in the course of my research for this book looked back on one item I did for *Look North* in 1984. My editor at the time, Roger Bufton, wanted me to explore some of the games we used to play in Yorkshire but were under threat. Like quoits.

Today the game is still played in parts of the county

although this seems to be mainly confined to pub leagues in parts of North Yorkshire. (There used to be a quoits ground outside the Plough Inn, Sleights.)

But in 1984, whilst not thriving, there was a competitive league in existence.

The game always seems to have been associated with rural life. Its origin, many claim, lies in Yorkshire, during the time of King John (1199-1216). But there are those who say it goes back to Roman times. I also heard recently a theory that the game was created when two Yorkshire farmers fell out and decided on the issue by seeing who could throw a horseshoe with the most accuracy.

In its original form it was played on a pitch. My *Look North* expert back in 1984 was Jim Miles. He described the game in the broadest Yorkshire I can ever remember hearing:

"The 'hob' or pin is a short metal rod, four and half inches high, set in the centre of a square yard of clay. Rest of pitch can be concrete or grass," he added.

A team consists of nine men, although some say it should be eleven.

I love the tradition which can only be Yorkshire in origin. The first pair do not toss a coin but a quoit and cry 'hill' or 'hole'. Each man (women were not allowed) throws two quoits, off a run of no more than two paces. A quoit that encircles the hob is called a 'ringer' and counts two points. However, if it is 'topped' or covered by your opponent, the two points are cancelled out and the 'topper' gets the points.

I uncovered other Yorkshire gems. A 'gater' is a quoit which stands in front of the hob and blocks an opponents throw. A 'Frenchman' is a quoit played on the right side of the hob, a 'pot' on the left.

Will it be a ringer, topper, gater, pot or Frenchman? Players look on as a quoit hurtles towards the hob during a quoits match at the village of Beckhole on the North York Moors.

How sad that this game is now confined to just a pub league.

In 1545 Roger Ascham declared that "quoiting was too vile for scholars". In that case, let's bring it back.

The Antient Scorton Silver Arrow

If Robin Hood did exist, then he must have come from Yorkshire. Wakefield claims him and there is a story that he is buried just off the M62 near Brighouse. Perhaps that explains why the oldest sporting event in the entire world, the Antient Scorton Silver Arrow, which dates back to 1673, comes from God's own county.

It is based around the village of Scorton in North Yorkshire but takes place at different venues with one stipulation: it must be in Yorkshire — although it has been allowed on occasions to venture into Lancashire!

It gave me another chance to visit the film archive to remind myself of this historic event. I was shocked to see that back in the 1980s I actually took part in it and hit the black spot in the centre of the target. No mean feat from a hundred yards. Mine was from ten.

Folklore has it that one Roger Ascham, tutor of Queen Elizabeth in the sixteenth century, actually provided the silver arrow, although there are countless more claimants to the honour. It is reported that part of the arrow has been dated to the sixteenth century with other parts to the seventeenth. What is fact is this. Every year it is competed for and the real arrow is on permanent display in the Royal Armouries in Leeds. To use a Yorkshire phrase, it is "definitely worth a few bob".

I love the tradition and organisation of it all. The title goes to the Captain of the Arrow. In practical terms this means that the captain gets to organise next year's

Ready, aim, fire! Archers line up to compete in the Antient Scorton Silver Arrow, the oldest sporting event in the world.

competition. It has changed little in one sense over the years but technology has had an influence. In 1948 a steel bow was introduced to replace the wooden one. More efficient and accurate, it became the bow to beat.

An excellent shot in the 2008 Antient Scorton Silver Arrow.

The event begins at 10am and is arranged with targets a hundred yards away at both ends. On the whistle the gentlemen shoot two arrows. They do the same when they have checked their scores.

I recall interviewing one competitor: "I only have two arrows. If I lose them I can't fire again." He lost them both and finished last.

One story for me sums up the wonderful tradition of the day. It happened back in 1948. A young twelve-year-old boy with a new lancewood bow turned up and asked if he could enter. The other gentlemen even doubted he'd get within ten yards of the target. To their astonishment he hit the gold circle and carried off the prize. No mean feat as there were some very decent archers competing.

This part of the competition lasts for two hours and, like at a cricket match, all stops for lunch. This can be a buffet or in some cases a three-course meal. Here comes the next tradition: all archers must have dined with the captain. If not they cannot shoot in the afternoon. Before that, however, the annual general meeting of the society takes place. Can you think of any other sporting event which stops in the middle for an AGM?

Another tradition also continues. Back in 1953 for the Coronation a telegram was sent to convey the archers' devotion to their monarch and the reply duly read out after lunch. No telegrams these days, so a rose is sent instead. I presume it is white. But the loyal toast continues.

After this rousing AGM, with plenty of wine and ale available for those who want it, all archers are invited back to the butts. It is said that many were out on their butts in recent times, but most get back to the action somehow. Safety concerns are paramount. Just as well really.

In recent years the event, which is taken very seriously by many competitors, has attracted wheelchair entrants — a new dimension to a truly great sporting tradition.

World Coal-Carrying Championship

OK, this may not be sport in the strictest sense of the word, but if you have ever been to this event you will know that it has all the ingredients. Brute strength. Determination. Humour. The latter in bucketloads ... or should that be sacks?

Gawthorpe, a small village just outside Ossett in West Yorkshire, may be an unlikely setting for a world championship, but it is a tough, uncompromising place where the local pit closed years ago.

The idea for the contest originated in the century-old

Beehive Inn and a chat between two local characters. Reggie Sedgwick and Amos Clapham, who was a local coal merchant, were enjoying a pint or two. In burst one Lewis Hartley who slapped Reggie on the back and uttered that famous Yorkshire greeting: "Tha looks knackered, lad" (or words to that effect).

"I am as fit as thee," said Reggie, "and if tha dun't believe me, gerra bag o' coil on thi back an Ah'll get one on mine, and Ah'll race thee up t' 'ill."

So in 1963 began the World Coal-Carrying Championship, a tradition which still takes place at Easter and draws a fair crowd. Admittedly it isn't what it used to be and that is because the mining industry in Yorkshire is no more.

In 1986 I covered the event and actually competed in part of the race. I completely knackered my back. Carrying a sack of coal is not easy, especially when you are a wimp like me. Actually, I did draw some praise from one person watching the event: " 'arry, tha's as much use as a chocolate fireguard. Leave it to t' experts and learn." I did.

Over the intervening years of its history the event has changed significantly and draws competitors from all over the north of England and Wales. Indeed, serious athletes take part now rather than miners and it is an event they want to win.

You would probably think that the best physical frame for success would be a big beefy person. Not so. As the years have gone by it is thought that the perfect weight is actually ten stone seven pounds with an athletic build. One farmer who regularly competes said that his training was deadly serious. "I don't have a sack of coal", he said, "but tatties [potatoes] instead."

*The World Coal-Carrying Championship is a tough event, and I
should know — when I competed in 1986 I knackered my back!
The photograph shows Chris Birkin (right) edging out Kevin
Sutcliffe to win the men's race in 2009.*

The rules are simple. Fifty kilos of coal (that's 110lb in
old money) have to be carried while running 1,000 metres
uphill. The winner takes the title King of the Coil
Humpers.

The event, which is mentioned in the *Guinness Book of Records*, is open to men and women. The world record is owned by David Jones of Meltham who ran the race in four minutes six seconds. He has done that twice. The women's record is five minutes five seconds. The holder, Julia Knight, is also from Meltham. Originally women only had to carry ten kilos (25lb) but in these enlightened times they carry the same weight and run the same distance as the men.

Like any major event the scrutiny before the race is precise. The coal is weighed accurately and then sewn up. This is done to stop competitors discarding some of the coal on the way. Usually the race begins at 12.30 with a press and media lorry in front. My cameraman in 1986 was a good friend of mine called Keith Massey and he focused on one guy with the sweat literally oozing out of him. It showed what energy was needed to complete the race. He completed fifty yards only. Yes, that was me. The coal was spilled over the road as I dropped out.

Only thirty competitors can take part in the main race because of safety concerns but there are now several other categories: under-fifteens, under-elevens and, wait for this, under-nines.

The World Coal-Carrying Championship is still a prize worth winning and the whole event, despite the decline of a once great industry, must be continued.

Fell running

I will have a go at most things, and in the twenty-seven years that I have been a performing seal (sorry, presenter) I have turned my hand to most of them. The hardest physical exertion, by some distance, was fell running. Way back in 1985 I entered the Buckden Fell Race. To say that I finished last would be an understatement, but I did finish.

Fell running is alive and kicking in God's own county, nowhere more so than Burnsall, one of my favourite places on earth. It's the gateway to so many great places in the Dales. The village holds its festivities during the feast of St Wilfrid, the patron saint of the church. So it is a moveable feast and race in every way.

The fell-running events attract the very best athletes in the country to the region. A few years ago I followed a group of Ghurka soldiers. They started as a squad and finished as one.

So what do you need to be a fell runner? Strength of course, but in my book one other ingredient is essential: bravery. Let me explain. When I ran the Buckden Fell Race in 1985, I was pretty fit. A regular runner, I knew I could run the distance with ease, but that didn't take account of the hills and the inclines. I was exhausted by the time I reached the top of the first hill. Then came the bravery. It was virtually a drop off the edge of a cliff in my book, but the expert runners were like goats. They launched themselves off the edge and ran full speed down the mountain. I went very gingerly.

Tradition has it that the Burnsall fell race can be traced back to 1870 when the idea was discussed in the Red Lion. Where better place to contemplate a crazy idea? It gets even more bizarre. The legend states that Tom Weston, a local character to say the least, tested the course one moonlit night and ran it naked. Now that is one test I would not be interested in. Then again…

After this the event became an annual one and the first report appeared in the *Craven Herald* back in 1882.

The most famous race may well have been back in 1910

*When the going gets tough ... a procession of fell runners snakes
up Penyghent during the Three Peaks Race.*

when a well-known Lakeland runner called Ernest H Dalzell set up the classic record for the event, running it in 12 minutes 59.8 seconds. Many questioned this time but a lot of people have verified it from reliable sources and even a descent time of 2 minutes 42 seconds was confirmed. The record stood until 1977 when a professional runner knocked ten seconds off it.

There's another reason why I would urge all fell runners to head for Burnsall: entry is free. It has to be, as the event takes place on open space. So all funds raised are from helpers who sell raffle tickets, run tombolas and so on.

The Three Peaks Race is clearly one notch (or is it three?) up the ladder of fitness. It is now a blue riband event and well established from the first race back in 1954 when only six souls entered.

Why anyone would want to run up Penyghent, Whernside and Ingleborough is probably one of life's great mysteries. The idea came from a Lancastrian called Fred Bagley. His time was two and a half hours to reach Ribblehead, and a further hour and twenty minutes to the Hill Inn to finish in a time of 3 hours 48 minutes.

Since then the time has tumbled dramatically and because of the popularity of the event the start point moved to Horton-in-Ribblesdale.

Ladies entered the race in 1979 when a well-known all-round cross country and cycling international, Jean Lochhead, finished the race in just over 3 hours 43 minutes.

For the record, one man won the race six years in a row: Jeff Norman. "I was allowed to enter when I was twenty-one", said Jeff, "and at first was happy just to finish. Then I won in 1970 and for the next five years after that."

Hugh Symonds enjoyed success in 1984, 1985 and 1986: "The sensation of crossing the line in Horton as the winner is probably the best feeling possible in fell racing. In fact I enjoyed my first win so much that I went straight to the pub and forgot the presentation. How embarrassing was that?"

Jean Rawlinson, winner in 1995, has a vivid recollection of her success:

"I climbed Whernside and overtook my main rival there. By the time I reached Ingleborough I was told I was way ahead. On reaching the final section I heard the race commentator announce that the first lady was about to enter the field. This brought a lump to my throat. I still cannot believe I won such a fantastic race."

Brendan Foster, one of the country's great athletes, once said to me that "great athletes may be judged by what they achieve on the track. But winning the Three Peaks, Buckden and Burnsall races is every bit as good as winning an Olympic medal." How true.

My favourite sporting quotes

Brian Clough on Eddie Gray, whose career was blighted by injuries: "If he had been a racehorse I would have had him shot."

Eric Morecambe: "You know when it is summer because you can hear the sound of leather hitting Brian Close."

Jim Mills, the legendary hard man of rugby league who was sent off over twenty times in his career: "People had suggested that I count to ten when my anger began to build up. But I could never get past three."

Freddie Trueman on Ian Botham: "He couldn't bowl a hoop down a hill."

Fred Trueman (again) being interviewed in Australia. Interviewer: "What do you think of our Sydney Bridge, Freddie?" Fred: "Your bridge? More like ours, lad. Built by Yorkshire firm Dorman and Long. And I bet tha still owes 'em money."

Gordon Strachan, the former Leeds United player, faced this question when he became the manager of Southampton. Reporter: "Tell me, Gordon, do you think you are the right man for the job?" Gordon: "No, definitely not. They should have given the job to George Graham. I am useless."

Brian Clough, the former Leeds United manager, about player-manager disagreements: "We talk about it for twenty minutes and then we all agree I was right."

Photographic acknowledgements

Fox family, pp48, 85, 88, 89; Getty Images, pp145 (Central Press), 159; Gration family, pp1, 4, 5, 20; Pete Hartley, p204; Kirklees Image Archive, pp161, 162, 163, 164; Press Association, pp66, 99 (Phil Noble), 100 (Matt Dunham), 112 (Rebecca Naden), 152 (S&G and Barratts/EMPICS Sport), 155 (David Jones), 159 (Tony Duffy/Allsport), 167 (S&G and Barratts/EMPICS Sport), 170 (S&G and Barratts/EMPICS Sport); Roger Keech, pp3, 6, 179; Mike Kipling, p195; Sheffield United FC, pp61, 62, 64; Sheffield Wednesday FC, pp42, 103, 104; Simon Miles, cover, p7; Society of Archers, pp197 (Tessa Emmerson), 198; Spencer family, pp121, 122 (Touchdown), 123, 124 (*Wellington Evening Post*), 125 (Perry Studios); Andrew Varley Picture Agency, pp9, 11, 15, 23, 24, 31, 34, 41, 52, 57, 77, 81, 108, 130, 133, 135, 137, 143, 146, 169, 175, 185, 189, 192, 201; Wakefield Wildcats RLFC, pp46, 47, 140, 141, 142; Yorkshire CCC Archives, pp14 (Ron Deaton Collection), 16, 19 (Michael O'Neill), 25 (Ron Deaton Collection), 27 (Ron Deaton Collection), 37 (*Yorkshire Post*/Ron Deaton Collection, 38 (*News Chronicle*/Ron Deaton Collection), 55 (Sporting Handbooks/Ron Deaton Collection), 59 (Sport & General Press Agency), 69 (Ron Deaton Collection), 75 (Walkers Studios/Ron Deaton Collection), 91 (Walkers Studios/Ron Deaton Collection), 93 (Ron Deaton Collection), 96, 111, 117 (Central Press Photos), 118 (Central Press Photos), 126, 128, 177 (Ron Deaton Collection), 180 (Ron Deaton Collection).

Whilst every effort has been made to trace copyright holders, the publishers would be pleased to correct any errors or omissions in future editions.

Index

INDEX